Tributes to
UNITY IN THE SPIRIT

"I highly recommend Ruth Ruibal's book as a valued instrument in God's hand toward the fulfillment of the prayer of our Lord in John 17. Her use of both Biblical and contemporary illustrations is most helpful."

> — *David Needham*
> *Professor, Multnomah School of the Bible*

"This book is not just about city transformation but about a martyr whose death paved the way for a breakthrough in Cali, Colombia. These stories are real and this woman has walked through the fire to produce this book. It is great for equipping pastors, leaders, and those interested in seeing cities impacted. It is a 'must read' for all city-reaching prayer intercessors."

> — *Frank Damazio*
> *Senior Pastor, City Bible Church, Portland*

"Ruth Ruibal's insightful and profound teaching on Biblical unity is both informative and penetrating. What she shares is explained with extraordinary insight…. Read this book and prepare to be challenged and informed on several key spiritual principles essential for authentic transformation on both a personal and a corporate level. This book pulsates with the heartbeat of God!"

> — *Alistair P. Petrie*
> *Executive Director, Sentinel Ministries/Canada*

"Ruth Ruibal has a special ability to share insights that teach, inspire and comfort the people of God. This wonderful resource not only tells the triumphant story of spiritual revolution in Cali, but points the way for impact in other cities as well. If you are looking for complex theories, you won't find them here. But if you are hungry for divine patterns of revival discovered through first-hand experience, I am pleased to recommend this book to you."

> — *David Cannistraci*
> *Senior Pastor, Evangel Christian Fellowship, San Jose*

UNITY
in the Spirit

UNITY
in the Spirit

Lessons from the Scriptures
and Life in Cali, Colombia

RUTH RUIBAL

TransformNations
media

A Division of The Sentinel Group
Lynnwood, Washington

Published by TransformNations Media,
A Division of The Sentinel Group
P.O. Box 6334
Lynnwood, WA 98036
www.TransformNations.com
All rights reserved.

PRINTED IN THE UNITED STATES OF AMERICA

ISBN: 1-930612-10-9

DEDICATION

To Julio Cesar Ruibal, beloved husband,
martyred on December 13, 1995
and now in the presence of our Lord;
a man who gave himself for God's purposes.

To Abby and Sarah, our daughters,
a great joy and delight to me,
my encouragement in the Lord,
my co-workers in the ministry.

To Ekklesia Christian Colombian Center
and the church of Jesus Christ in Cali, in Colombia,
and throughout the world—especially to those
who have suffered for the Gospel.

And most of all, to our Lord Jesus,
our Life and Comforter,
Who counted the cost and paid the price
that we might have abundant life.

TABLE OF CONTENTS

Foreword

I had just sauntered into the auditorium and settled in the back row. Having raced from the airport, I began collecting my thoughts, tuning up to minister at yet another conference. My friend George Otis, Jr., whose Sentinel Group ministry had sponsored the gathering, was introducing a woman I had seen on the critically acclaimed *Transformations* video. Within moments I was transfixed as this woman spoke. As I listened, I soon realized that I was not hearing the ordinary material one hears on the conference circuit. A penetrating sense of God's presence and wonder seemed to resonate in her words.

Ruth Ruibal spread before us a feast of divine wisdom. Her teaching was not only eloquent but also saturated with understanding. An unusual authority sounded through her words, her teaching the obvious overflow of her deep communion with God. Here was a woman who had forged an understanding of His ways in the crucible of Cali, Colombia, one of the most challenging and dangerous spots in the Western Hemisphere.

As she spoke, it seemed that a gracious ferocity pulsated through her entire being, her intensity fueled by one of her primary passions: *the unity of the Body of Christ.*

I was convicted. I was refreshed. I was brought low before the Almighty's throne. I was cuddled in my Heavenly Father's arms. Rarely have I felt so warmly humbled as I did that afternoon when I heard this prophetic messenger from Cali.

Since that time I have had the privilege of partnering with Ruth in a number of conferences and we have found ourselves both deeply concerned over the church's lack of understanding of the ways of God. What Ruth gives us in this book is one of the best, most comprehensive sets of teachings on unity ever expressed on the printed page. For what she and scores of pastors in Cali have discovered about unity covers ground rarely traveled by many of us in North America. These chapters are more than timely words. They provide a roadmap of how churches in a city can become The Church in the City; how pastors can truly bond with one another and labor together; how the plagues of jealousy, criticism and competition can be conquered.

A.W. Tozer once said that Psalm 133 describes for us the dynamics of genuine revival. Throughout the Psalm, God takes every initiative, promising to bless His people with the fullness of His presence. The only requirement of us is that we dwell together in unity.

Ruth has put her finger on this one requirement: *maintaining unity in the bond of peace.* If unity is the key by which our cities can experience the unparalleled presence of God, then by all means we must heed these words, learn His ways—and by His grace let God transform our cities.

—*Steve Fry*
Songwriter/Author

PREFACE

In 1968, after receiving my master's degree in public health from Columbia University, I came to Cali to serve as a visiting professor in the master's program at the Universidad del Valle, the state university. I worked with both professionals and students, with the higher strata of society and with the poor—whites, blacks, indigenous peoples, and *mestizos* (mixed races of the different ethnic backgrounds). My work took me throughout the southern and western portions of the country. And I love it all. I love the cities as well as the countryside—the mountains, jungles, valleys, coastlines and plains. Colombia is a beautiful country and its people just enhance its beauty. The Lord called me here when I was only seven years old, and I believe the Lord gave me His own love for this country.

The university was my mission field. I began to speak to people about the Lord, and by the end of that first year we had formed a small group that met regularly. By 1969, we had established the first nondenominational charismatic church in the city; it is still operating today.

In 1973, while leading this small church and serving the Lord as a short-term consultant for the World Health Organization/Pan American Health Organization, I met Julio Cesar Ruibal. I first read about him on the front pages of *El Tiempo*, the most prestigious newspaper in the country. The article told how a young Bolivian was holding massive crusades in stadiums and coliseums under the auspices of a well-known charismatic Roman Catholic priest, Padre Rafael Garcia Herreros. During Julio's three-day crusade in Cali, my faith was challenged to grow as never before; I saw for myself the miracles and healings that were taking place.

Julio and I were married in 1976 and spent our first year in Portland, Oregon, studying in Multnomah School of the Bible's graduate program and taking night courses at Portland Bible College. At the end of the year we returned to Colombia with our first baby, Abigail. The year before I had turned the church that I started in Cali over to others, so Julio and I began a new work. In 1978 we founded Ekklesia Centro Cristiano Colombiano (Ekklesia Colombian Christian Center) with a vision to some day have a school, college, communications center, health clinic and other aspects of ministry.

Cali has now been my home for more than half my life. It was here that I met my husband. It was here that we raised our children and established a church. It was here that my husband was martyred. And today, it is the place where my daughters and I have chosen to remain.

It would be a great privilege and delight for me to relate the story of God's move in this city. However, I believe that an attempt to tell Cali's story would at best present the reader with only pieces of the truth, a biased report, that would limit the wonderful story in which the Lord has worked for us. No one except the Lord knows the whole story. However, I can share something very close to my heart, something experienced in Cali in a special way: unity in the Spirit.

In defining unity, along with all the misconceptions and difficulties associated with it, I use examples from what I have seen and experienced. These are only pieces of the story, intended to clarify the point I am making. They are not the whole "Cali Story." Others have played a far more significant role than I have in the Lord's work here. I pray that the Lord will grant understanding in this matter to the reader.

Purposefully, I have left out the names of pastors and Christian leaders, with the exception of three presidents of the Association of Evangelical Ministers (ASMICEV): Alfonso Diaz (1995–1996), Roosevelt Muriel (1997–1998), and Julian Collazos (1999–2000).* The Lord has used these men, the Association's board of directors, and the whole body of Christ in Cali to accomplish His work. Each person and ministry has worked according to the call and ministry given by God.

Many other organizations and ministries have walked with us and strengthened our hands. For example, The Latin-American Foundation for Theological Studies (FLET) has helped with continuing education for the pastors and leaders. Christ for the City, under Ramon Cardona, Youth with a Mission, and many others have stood with us. Pastors Randy and Marcy MacMillan have brought gifted teachers and worship ministries to Cali from the USA. All of these servants, and many others besides, have greatly blessed and strengthened the city-church, even though they are not mentioned in the following chapters. In a very real sense, they have helped make this book possible.

I wish to thank all those who were most directly involved in bringing this book into existence. My daughter Sarah closely accompanied me through each step, typing and editing and being with me as a very special prayer partner. Craig and Marilyn Smith helped by graciously opening their home to me, providing a quiet, peaceful place to pray and write. John and Carol Juliano first suggested that I write this book and encouraged me along the way; they have been faithful friends throughout, and Carol was a special blessing in the editing process. Chuck Train and Chuck DeRenzo, members of the board of directors of the Ruibal Ministries, prayed for this book to become a reality. Alistair Petrie and Steve Fry gave me valuable and timely suggestions for the book during our ministry trips. George Otis, Jr. and The Sentinel Group have encouraged me and given me the great privilege of taking this book as the first in their new publishing line. Not least, I extend a very sincere thanks to all the intercessors that have stood with me in prayer through some very difficult times.

To God be the glory for what He has done, for what He is doing, and for what is yet to come. He is the Sovereign Lord.

Names, dates and events are current to the time of the writing of this book.

INTRODUCTION

Unity and city transformation are becoming more common subjects within the church today. However, these are easier topics to talk about than to accomplish. Although there is a growing desire in the hearts of many Christians for unity, I have found that one of the greatest problems hindering it, next to pride, is a lack of understanding of just what it is, how it functions, and why it is important—its purpose. There are many misconceptions, so we need to understand what the Bible teaches about unity as we continue to fulfill our Lord's desire "that they may be one...."

Cali became infamous because of the Cali cartel and the drug lords who ran it. Later, after the *vigilias* (all night prayer meetings) started, Cali became an inspiration because of the move of God. This change has become well known through the *Transformations* video produced by The Sentinel Group.

I met George Otis, Jr. for the first time in 1998, when he came to Cali to research what the Lord was doing in our city. Mr. Otis made the video to encourage intercessors. He wanted to show how the Lord has answered prayer in different cities throughout the world. He thought that 5,000 videos would be sufficient, but it went far beyond his greatest dreams. As I write this book, 150,000 videos have been distributed. It has been translated into about 40 languages and has gone into some 150 countries and been seen by as many as 50 million viewers. The video has encouraged Christians throughout the world.

At the time the *Transformations* video was made, just eight cities were known to George Otis, Jr. as "transformed." Now it is estimated that there are more than one hundred. God is doing an awesome thing in our day and people are hungry to hear the good news. And the movement is now spreading to whole regions, as documented in *Transformations II: The Glory Spreads.* This sequel, released in the summer of 2001, shares the stories of God's transforming power in Uganda and the High Arctic where the fire of God is sweeping through entire provinces and national homelands.

In select areas conversion rates are spiking at between 70–90 percent of the population. God is also moving in unprecedented ways in Russia's far-eastern Chukotka Peninsula.

These developments are exciting for almost anyone. Yet an emotional response will not produce unity nor city transformation. Christians with a desire and vision for transformation need to understand the principles that are to be followed, and the cost it will take to achieve their goal.

The first section of this book is meant to help provide a definition of unity, based on biblical references as well as from some of our experiences in Cali. We began our journey into unity with the first *vigilia* in March 1995. At the end of that year, my husband died as a martyr for the Lord Jesus Christ. At his funeral we made a covenant of unity that stands today, a covenant that is written on our hearts.

The covenant we made gave us a good foundation on which to walk; however, we also discovered that more is needed. To continue and grow in unity we must walk in humility, holiness, and obedience; we must persevere in prayer, grow through trials, and have a vision that incorporates the invisible, eternal purposes of God. The second section of this book goes further into these things.

It was the middle of 1995 that the Lord began to teach me more fully that unity is not an end in itself, but rather a means to an end. Unity in the spirit not only produces immediate blessings but is also necessary for the full purposes of God to be accomplished on the face of the earth.

The *Transformations* video tells the story of carrots the size of a man's forearm in Almolonga, Guatemala. Every time I see this image, the Lord reminds me that His thoughts and ways are higher than our own. It is God's way of saying to me, "Don't settle for what man calls 'normal.' Don't settle for less than what I have in mind." One of the goals of unity is to show the world just who our God is—in large part through a lifestyle that provides answers for a lost world. The last chapter, which I have placed in a separate section because of its importance, addresses the long-term goal of unity.

My desire with this book is to encourage readers to walk in unity. Through practical examples of unity at work, I believe the reader will be able to understand the steps needed to see God move in our own communities and regions—and to avoid some of the pitfalls along the way. I pray that this book will plant a vision in the heart of the reader and become a blessing and encouragement to many.

And this gospel of the kingdom will be preached in the world as a testimony to all nations....
— Matthew 24:14

Part I

Stepping Into
UNITY

The Common Starting Place

We weren't fighting, exactly,
but we weren't walking in unity either.

It was still dark that August morning in 1995. Julio and I were seated in the Pascual Guerrero Stadium, well known for the many soccer games it hosted in Cali, Colombia. However, this night was different; the stadium now held 40,000 people for a *vigilia* (all-night united prayer meeting). Just five months earlier we had met in the Coliseo del Pueblo, the local coliseum, packed out by some 20,000 people. But now we were in the stadium with twice that number. We were seated on the running track with the pastors and their families, surrounded by tens of thousands in the bleachers. It was the first time that so many Christians had come together to seek the Lord for the salvation of our city. Praying with such a large company of believers was exhilarating in itself, but what made it an especially awesome night was the wonderful, powerful, and almost palpable presence of God.

But it was not always like this. Just a few years before, the churches in Cali were like churches elsewhere. We weren't fighting, exactly, but we weren't walking in unity either. We worked independently, each church with its own programs. Even society looked on the evangelical church as weak and fragmented. And since there were so few professionals among our members, outsiders considered the churches to be made up of poor, uneducated and deceived people. Evangelical Christianity simply had not made inroads into society, a job that is especially difficult when Christians aren't walking together.

In the late 70s the evangelical pastors of Cali formed ASMICEV (Evangelical Christian Ministers' Association of the Valley). Julio helped them write the organization's bylaws and became an active member of its board of directors. The number of churches was so small that the meager files fit easily into a single carton, kept in the home of the pastor who was president at the time.

Although it was a far cry from what the Bible calls unity, we did manage to make some progress through the Ministers' Association. We were few in number but the Lord helped us organize evangelistic crusades and other projects. But as soon as the activity was over, we were back in our individual churches.

Our most outstanding achievement during those early years was establishing the first Christian political party in the history of Colombia. However, Christians didn't want to vote for someone who didn't come from their church or denomination. As a result, we weren't able to win any seats in city government. But at least Christians in Cali began to realize that we could, and perhaps should, participate in city affairs.

By the mid-80s, however, Julio and I ran into problems that eventually separated us from the Ministers' Association. Through these difficulties, we learned lessons that changed our lives.

Disappointed by Brothers

A student in our Bible college became part of our youth group's leadership team. Julio had led the young man, a foreign student I'll call "Roberto," to the Lord. Now the young man was studying to prepare himself for the ministry. But as the months went by, we discovered that Roberto had a problem that was affecting others; it was serious enough for us to remove him from the leadership team until we could work with him and lead him to victory in this area of his life.

To our surprise, Roberto was unreceptive to this simple correction. He took his case to a pastor friend of ours, who sided with him without making further inquiries from the leadership of our college or church. Soon the whole situation was blown completely out of proportion. Then the pastor somehow obtained the Ministers' Association's letterhead without the leadership's knowledge and secretly sent a letter to our supporters. On the Ministers' Association's stationery, he claimed that the Association did not want the Ruibals in Cali.

When our supporters informed us what had happened, Julio went directly to the Ministers' Association for help. But lacking experience with this sort of thing, they were unsure how to handle the case. In all likelihood, they probably considered it to be more of a squabble between two churches. They eventually decided to write a letter disclaiming any part in the letter that had accused us and expressing support for our ministry. However, the letter of disclaimer was delayed for many weeks and Julio decided that he shouldn't insist that the Association help. After several months, Julio wrote to our supporters himself, addressing the situation.

Under the circumstances, Julio did not feel that he could continue with the Ministers' Association any longer; they were what he called "inoperative." Greatly disappointed, and probably feeling somewhat betrayed, he resigned from the Association. He loved these men and did not consider them his enemies, yet we were no longer working together as we had before this incident.

About a year or so later, Julio received a visit from the pastor who had supported Roberto. He asked Julio to forgive him and added, "I only pray that the Lord will not put someone in my life to do the same to me as I did to you." Julio forgave him, the two embraced, and their friendship was restored.

A Story Repeated

Unfortunately, I have heard similar stories in city after city, and country after country. In an attempt to walk together, problems and misunderstandings arise, and leaders become offended. Not knowing just how to react, and many times with an honest desire not to make things worse, we pull back to a more comfortable place. However, without realizing it, we are only adding to the problem.

Most of us have ideas about unity and a desire to see unity between the Christian leadership and believers in our city. We know that this is the will of God, for Jesus prayed that we would be one, yet we seldom see unity in action. Part of the problem is that we lack an understanding of what unity really is.

Definition of Unity

Cooperation is only a step towards unity.

One of the first times the Bible mentions unity is a negative example found in Genesis 11. The people of that time were constructing a city and tower "for themselves"—to "make a name" for themselves. This interested God. The Bible says that the LORD came down to see the city and tower. The people were one, spoke one language, and had one purpose: to make a name for themselves through their building project. The conclusion given by the Lord lays out an important principle related to unity: "Nothing they plan to do will be impossible for them."

Now if nonbelievers found that nothing would be impossible to them through unity, how much more is this true for the people of God? What if we were one, speaking one language and having one purpose—"thy kingdom come, thy will be done"? Then we would have God the Father, Son and Holy Spirit, along with all the heavenly angels, on our side! Nothing would be impossible for us! No wonder the enemy fights unity so much! The enemy's tactic is always to divide and conquer.

Unfortunately, we are very vulnerable and gullible. Within the local church we can become divided over the color of the walls or carpet, the location of a church sign, and countless other nonessential issues. And we have allowed different styles of worship and minor doctrinal differences to separate us from other churches. We allow small offenses to separate us from the body of Christ. The enemy knows that if the people of God would walk in unity, the purposes of God would be accomplished—that nothing would be impossible for us. Unfortunately, many of God's own people don't understand that principle.

Psalm 133 is another Scripture that is commonly thought of in relation to unity. Anyone who has been to Cali sees that unity is very "good" and very "pleasant"; the anointing and refreshing are present. It is almost palpable. The last verse in this Psalm teaches us that where there is unity there is also a command from the Lord, a command for blessing and salvation. Just as the Lord commanded there to be light, and there was light, so He commands that blessing and salvation flow whenever we walk together in unity.

We have experienced this increasingly over the last years in Cali. As the result of unity, there are so many people coming to the Lord that our problem is trying to properly disciple the new converts. In our own local church experience, we finally came to the conclusion that every person in the church needed either to be in the process of being discipled or involved in discipling others. The influx is just too great to allow us to do otherwise. Where there is unity, there is anointing, refreshing, blessing, and salvation.

Cooperation: A First Step Towards Unity

A common misunderstanding among Christians is to think that cooperation is the same as unity. Typically a large group of churches in a given community come together to support an evangelistic crusade or some other Christian event. They work together with the organization: counseling, ushering, following up on decisions for Christ, and so forth. But when the crusade or event is over, everyone returns to his own church until another Christian event takes place. This is cooperation, a coming together around an event. It can remain as such, or it can deepen into real unity.

Unity Seen in the Tribes of Israel

Israel offers one of the most outstanding examples of unity found in the Bible. Israel was one nation with the same culture, language, and destiny. She was set apart as a different people, a people that would reflect Jehovah to the surrounding heathen nations, causing them to want to know Israel's wonderful God. As Jeremiah records in chapter 33, verse 9, *"...this city (Israel) will bring Me renown, joy, praise, and honor before all nations on earth that hear of all the good things I do for it...."* Israel's life was to provoke the other nations to want Israel's God.

Israel, however, was made up of 12 tribes, each with a different calling, its own special anointing or gifting, that reflected a particular aspect of God's manifest character. For example, Issachar was to reflect the wisdom of God. Dan was to reflect the justice of God through his judgments. Judah reflected praise, and so forth. All the tribes had wisdom from God, but Issachar had an anointing above the other tribes for this particular aspect of God's character. Likewise, all the tribes were to praise God, but Judah had a special anointing in this area.

If the nations surrounding Israel had seen only one of the 12 tribes, their conclusions about God would have been unbalanced. They would never have seen the fuller expression of God's character —only a partial and unbalanced view. But if they saw all the tribes together as one nation, they would have a more complete picture of the God served by the Israelites.

A Family Example

The family offers another very practical example of unity. My daughters are so different that at times Julio and I would ask how it was possible for them to come from the same parents. Even in very large families, parents don't find their children to be alike, nor would we want them to be alike; each child is different. And because our children are all different, one compliments and polishes the other. They become richer as they learn from one another. They appreciate one another for what each one has, rather than criticize one another for what each lacks. I believe this is also the delight of our Father when He looks at His children.

We all enjoy a good melody, but what can compare to a philharmonic orchestra, in which many different instruments take part? Why would we ever want or even try to make our church like another? The Lord has made us unique in order to show a fuller, richer reflection of Himself through our community.

Some New Testament References

In Romans 12 and 1 Corinthians 12, Paul uses the example of the human body to describe how we function together. Although some parts are seen and others are not, all parts are necessary for optimal functioning. The body grows and builds itself as *each part* does its work (Ephesians 4).

The Apostle Peter picks this up in 1 Peter 2:4–10. We are called a "spiritual house." A house is only considered useful when all its elements are in place and functioning: walls, floors, ceilings, foundation. If anything is missing, the house is not complete, and not as functional as it should be.

Peter also calls us "a royal priesthood." We read in Numbers 3:21–37, each family was called to perform specific duties for which they alone had responsibility. The families of Gershon took care of the curtains of the courtyard and entrance. The families of Kohath took care of the ark, the table of the Presence, the lampstand, the altars, the articles used for ministering in the sanctuary, and the curtain covering the ark. The families of Merari took care of the frames of the tabernacle, its crossbars, posts, bases, and tent pegs. If any of these families had gotten tired of its duties and tried to take over another's responsibilities, there would have been chaos. In fact, Israel would have been unable to follow the cloud by day and the pillar of fire by night. Similarly, when we don't appreciate and respect the unique call upon each church, we find it difficult to follow the Lord's guidance in our communities.

Diversity is a Necessary Ingredient of Unity

Peter calls us "a holy nation, a peculiar people." Obviously, no nation or people is made up of individuals who are exactly alike. A house, a priesthood, a nation, and a people all involve unity with great diversity. In fact, true unity demands diversity; otherwise, it would be uniformity, not unity.

Today, the gifts and calling of God for each church are unique. One church may be anointed in praise and worship. Another may be called to focus more sharply on strengthening the family, or education. Yet another may be anointed to minister to the poor. All churches function to some degree in each of these areas, but they also have one or two areas in which they excel, depending on the calling and anointing that the Lord has given them.

A Picture of Unity

One morning while fasting and praying, I asked the Lord to teach me more about unity. Immediately He impressed on my spirit Habakkuk 2:14:

For the earth will be filled with the knowledge of the glory of the LORD, as the waters cover the sea.

At the same time, I saw a vision of a large lake with many tributaries flowing into it from all sides. Then the waters began to rise and, as they did, the tributaries began to overflow their banks. Finally the waters rose so high that all the tributaries merged together into one vast body of water, covering the area completely. At that point, one could fill a pail with water and not know the water's origin. It made no difference, for the waters covered the sea as the knowledge of the glory of the Lord covered the earth—and that alone was important!

God Uses Whoever He Wants

As we walk in unity we enjoy open doors without knowing whom God is using to open them. It does not really matter—not if we want to see the Lord's glory in our communities.

For example, here in Cali, the State University Hospital shut its doors to the gospel; pastors were not allowed in to minister to the sick. There were some 60 Christian employees out of more than 1,000 at the hospital, but the Christians were not allowed to meet together or have any kind of Christian activities.

Our church was visited by a missions team from Lewiston, Idaho, in the summer of 1999. They were trained in the creative arts and worked with our RC (Rhythm of Christ) dance troop.[1] A nurse from my church, who works in the hospital, was able to arrange an invitation for the RC and the Idaho team to come to the hospital.

That day, as the youth were leaving the hospital, the medical director was entering. The nurse introduced them and the director asked if he could have an appointment with them the following day. This man had been raised and trained in Cuba and was a

---

[1] 1 Our local church has formed a hip-hop (street dancing) evangelism troop called RC, Rhythm of Christ. The young people involved in this ministry probably spend more time in prayer and intercession than they do in practice. Any one of them can give a Gospel message anywhere they go and their lives back up their words.

proclaimed atheist. His father, a former guerrilla leader in Colombia, had taken refuge in Cuba after participating in the burning of the Justice Palace in the 1980s.

The next day, when we went into the meeting, a Christian administrator and two Christian nurses met with us as well. The medical director began the meeting by explaining his situation to the youth. Everything was negative: the hospital needed funds, equipment, personnel, etc. At the end, he asked if there were any questions. A young man from Idaho asked, "If everything is so negative, why are you here?" The director answered, "My brother and I have a *commitment* to serve in this city and to see it improve. I am here to direct a hospital that will run without illicit money, without political influence, and to give good care to the patients. That is my dream and I am committed to it."

I spoke up and said that that was the heart of God as well. Then I left this challenge, "Sir, this morning I was praying for you and the hospital. As I prayed, the Lord put it on my heart to tell you that if you will open the doors of the hospital to the gospel, not only will the patients improve but this hospital will not shut down due to lack of funds. The Lord will supply your needs."

He thanked me. Then a young person asked if he would mind if they prayed for him. He agreed but was uncomfortable; he didn't know if he should kneel, stand, or just what. The young people told him to stay seated and asked, "Can we lay hands on you?" Again the director replied affirmatively. They gathered around him, praying briefly for him. At the end, the doctor ran out of the room without a word. Later we discovered that he had run into his office and told his secretary that no one had ever prayed for him before and that he didn't know what he was supposed to do.

After a couple of weeks passed, we were informed that the medical director had assigned a meeting room to the Christian employees. Next he opened the doors of the hospital for Christian ministry. God had performed another miracle.

The Christian administrators and nurses invited all the churches to participate and organized a training session for hospital visitation for those interested. And now, at the time of writing this book, we have city church teams going in every day to minister on every ward in the hospital. We have received many testimonies of healing through their ministry. The visitation teams meet every month with different pastors of the city to receive ministry and encouragement.

Few would know that the Lord used our team to reach the director's heart. Perhaps there were other churches that had interceded for this situation. If so, they did more work than we did. It really makes no difference.

The more we work together as one body, the less we assign credit with names. The point is that the Lord is opening doors and uses whomever He wishes. Who are we that we should try to take any credit for what the Lord has done? I am well aware of the fact that I enjoy many open doors because of the other pastors and brethren who have prayed, believed, and acted in obedience to the Lord. It doesn't matter what their names are or what they did. The Lord keeps the records as He sees fit. We find our fulfillment in being obedient to His will and direction. *"All that we have accomplished you have done for us"* (Isaiah 26:12b). And that is what unity is all about—seeing His kingdom come and His will being done, on earth as it is in heaven.

Learning to Speak Unity

In the process of walking together, we learn to speak differently as well. In 1 Corinthians 1 we read about divisions centering on the issue of credit for conversions. Some claimed to be of Peter, others of Apollos, and yet others of Paul. However, one said, "I am of Christ," seeming to understand that only Christ could save. But that answer only added to the disunity. The answer that would have brought unity was, "WE are of Christ." This simple answer could have brought the divisions to an end. And today, if we are going to have true unity, we need to think beyond our own individual lives and churches and realize that we are only a part of a larger whole.

Our Weakness, Another's Strength

The Lord has strategically placed specific churches in our localities so that together we can reflect the glory of God's character to the community. As I walk with the brethren, my weaknesses will be covered by their strengths; likewise, my strengths will cover their weaknesses. In fact, the Lord created us with weaknesses and strengths so that we would need to be united in order to fulfill His purposes.

Pride, however, causes us to isolate ourselves so that no one will see our weaknesses. Then, in order to show off our strengths, we begin to criticize those who don't have our same strengths. We don't understand that those dear brethren were never meant to have our strengths; as we walk together as one, they have that strength through us! Together we make a whole.

When we truly understand this, and the Holy Spirit engraves it on our hearts, then we appreciate others and competition begins to fade away. We realize that none of us can do the job alone and we need each other. I begin to realize that I cannot be or do all that the Lord has for me unless I am walking with the other brethren. God is working through His *united* church to bring the community to the knowledge of Jesus Christ.

Examples from Cali

In Cali, there is a ministry with a call and gifting to work with drug addicts. The ministry has a program of restoration and has formed a church. If, in any given church in our city, a new convert has a problem with addiction, we can lead the person to the Lord, disciple him, baptize him in water and cast out demons if necessary. But, as anyone experienced dealing with drug addiction knows, that person can grow much more quickly in the Lord with stricter boundaries and accountability. For this reason, whenever a person with an addictive background comes to the Lord through our ministry, we send him to the other church where he can receive more adequate help. We let him know that he needs that kind of ministry for his first steps in the Lord. When he is restored, he may stay at that church, return to ours, or go to a church closer to his home. The bottom line is that he needs to attend a local church.

The objective isn't to fill our pews, but to offer the best possible follow-up, grounding a person in the faith and allowing him to grow in the Lord. If, with a desire for church growth, I were to insist that our church start a ministry for these people, I would cause more problems than solutions. Perhaps I could even train members of the church for this ministry, but in the end, if the Lord has not called us to this work, they will be frustrated by my effort to force round pegs into square holes. The Lord calls and equips us for the ministries that He has given us. Each church has different callings. Together we can effectively minister to the community according to His plan and purpose. Some sow, others water, and yet others reap, but we all rejoice in the harvest, and God receives the glory because it is He that gives the increase (1 Corinthians 3:3–8).

Likewise, if another church is going to have an evangelistic outreach, they will frequently ask our RC hip-hop team to go with them. And the team gladly goes with that church to bless their ministry. We don't charge anything for it, nor do we expect to get any of the decision cards afterwards. We are there to serve that church and to help them accomplish what God has called them to do.

We Need a Revelation

I like to think of the body of Christ as a wheel in which we are the spokes and God is the hub. If we try to make unity happen by drawing closer to each other, some spokes will be grouped closely together while others will be separated by large gaps. Thrown out of balance, the wheel will wobble. But if we each draw closer to the Lord, we will be automatically drawn closer together. Then, as a perfectly balanced wheel, we can roll forward with momentum.

Often, after seeing what the Lord is doing through unity in different communities, leaders will decide to "do" unity and community transformation in their area. But unity isn't something we "do." It is a revelation from God. That is why Paul prayed that the Ephesian church would be given "the Spirit of wisdom and revelation, so that you may know Him better. I pray also that the eyes of your heart may be enlightened in order that you may know ...the riches of His glorious inheritance in the saints..." (Ephesians 1:17, 18). Once unity has been revealed to us by the Holy Spirit, we think and act differently. It is automatically expressed in our lifestyle. It is similar to love. Both unity and love are confirmed by their fruits. "I love you" doesn't mean much apart from actions that demonstrate that love. Yet, at the same time, those actions may be repeated by someone else without being motivated by love. Likewise, unity is a matter of the heart.

Unity Deepens with Time

As time passed, unity deepened in our hearts. We saw an expression of this growth in the March for Jesus. In our first march in 1995, the president of the Ministers' Association asked us to make banners with all sorts of messages uplifting the name of Christ. At the bottom of each banner was the name of the participating church, and each church marched out from our meeting in alphabetical order. Halfway through the march, Julio and I noted that the congregations had mixed together. Even though the banner had the name of a particular church, the people from other congregations were marching under it.

A few years later, the Lord had knit our hearts together even more. The president of the Ministers' Association was explaining the logistics of the march, asking the churches to make banners with clear messages uplifting the name of Jesus. "And," he added, "on the lower portion of the banner, you can place the name of your church." The whole room broke out in bedlam, and the same message was shouted out by pastors in different parts of the room:

"We don't want to put the name of our church on our banners!"

"We are one church!"

"Why would we want to put the name of our church on a banner when we are one?"

The message was clear and the president had to take back his suggestion. Unity had reached our hearts without anyone conscientiously realizing what had happened.

An Expression of the Kingdom of God

Unity is an indispensable expression of the kingdom of God and a means of salvation for a community. If the world can see it working, then it will be drawn to the Savior who makes it possible. We find unity as we lose ourselves in the Lord. Jesus makes this clear when He prays *"that all of them may be one, Father, just as You are in Me and I am in You"* (John 17: 21). That is true unity. To the degree that we die to self and lose ourselves in Him, we will find unity not only with Him, but also with one another.

Preparation for Unity

You have no right to be offended.

The study of unity is easy, but the practice of unity is another thing. The process is not smooth. It can produce a noisy rattling at first, much like the dry bones that came to life in the prophet Ezekiel's vision (chapter 37). How easy unity would be if we were all mature, complete, perfect Christians! But none of us has yet reached perfection, and that means we are going to have problems. We are all in the process of growing and maturing, and in the process we are going to make mistakes. In the process someone may even take advantage of another. The question is not what happens *if* someone takes advantage of me, but rather how will I respond *when* someone takes advantage of me?

We can decide before the problem presents itself. Jesus prayed in John 17:22, 23:

I have given them the glory that You gave Me, that they may be one as We are one: I in them and You in Me. May they be brought to complete unity to let the world know that You have sent Me and have loved them even as You have loved Me.

Jesus says that the Father gave Him glory and Jesus passed that glory on to us for the specific purpose that we might be one. It takes the glory of God to be able to walk together in unity. We cannot do it by human effort; we must have the glory of God to do so. We can choose to receive that glory from Him.

Need for Patience

I often remember our daughter Abby's first steps. Julio was on one side of the room with Abby, and I was on the other. I called Abby to come to me. She took only a few steps and managed to get part way across the room. We were absolutely delighted at her feat. Why? Because as parents, we knew the baby would soon make it all the way across the room. In the same way, our heavenly Father rejoices at the steps we take. However, as a church we are often impatient with our fellow Christians' achievements; instead of delighting in their progress, we are critical of them for not getting there fast enough! Yet when it comes to ourselves, we seem to use a different measure.

Why do we leave room for error in ourselves and not in others? Probably because we see our motives as right, but we question those of our fellow Christians. Basically, the problem is pride. We must allow others to grow at the pace that God has given them. God is sovereign and can deal with others as patiently as He deals with us. We are all still growing.

Our Process

In Cali, almost five years went by before the Lord was able to get His message of unity into our hearts. In the fall of 1991, Julio and I went to a health clinic in Strongsville, Ohio, where we fasted for approximately three weeks. Although we frequently went on spiritual fasts, this time was different; it was our first therapeutic fast. We were amazed to see its physical as well as spiritual benefits. Near the end of the fast, the Lord began speaking to Julio about the need for reconciliation and unity. As he read the Scriptures, verses from the Beatitudes seemed to leap off the page. They spoke of forgiveness and the Lord being kind to all, even to the unthankful and wicked. Finally, Julio turned to me and said, "Honey, I have to forgive the Ministers' Association. Yes, I'm going to go back and tell them that I forgive them."

Before I could respond, the Holy Spirit spoke to Julio, "Oh, no you won't! You'll ask them to forgive you!"

"What, Lord?" Julio asked. "They are the ones that offended me. Why should I ask forgiveness of them?"

Again the Lord responded in His own unnerving way, "That's just it. You were offended, but as a Christian you have no right to be offended. By taking on an offense, you offended them. You must reflect Me. You must ask forgiveness for not reflecting My character, My person, when you left the Association."

The Lord was dealing with Julio from a whole different viewpoint. Julio knew that he had to ask forgiveness—not for being offended, for that would only cast blame on the others. No. He had to ask forgiveness for offending them. By leaving the Ministers' Association, he had offended them. His sin was that he had not reflected the One he loved so much by taking on an offense himself. In this way, he would learn to reflect our precious Savior who, being reviled, reviled not, who knew how to walk in obedience to His Father, no matter what man did to Him.

When we got back to Colombia in late 1991, Julio went directly to the pastors to ask forgiveness and to tell them that he should never have left the Ministers' Association. The response was overwhelming. He was forgiven and received with open arms. Julio told me later, "If I had known how wonderful reconciliation is, I would have done this a long time ago." Before long, Julio was once again an active member of the Association's board of directors.

By this time, Roberto had settled down, married a lovely Christian girl and was starting a family. He had grown, and so had the church he started. Julio called him, and Roberto was restored to fellowship.

From then on, the message that Julio bore was that of unity. He spoke to the pastors about it, preached it in the church, and talked about it everywhere he went. The message of unity was written on his heart—not just a message of cooperation. At that point, as pastors in Cali, we hadn't gone beyond cooperation and so it was a hard message to grasp. We needed the revelation from the Lord for that.

The Situation in Cali

In the meantime, Cali had fallen into a desperate situation. It was becoming infamous for its drug cartel, one of the best-organized criminal organizations in the world. Because of the murders, kidnappings, torture and such, the international press considered Colombia "the most violent country in the world," other than countries at war. And Cali had the reputation for being the most violent city in Colombia.

The drug lords became more powerful every day. They infiltrated almost every sector of society. They bribed the justice system, the political system, the police force, the anti-drug forces. They also brought violence, prostitution, corruption, witchcraft, torture, and fear with them.

Cali seemed to be prosperous as drug lords laundered their money through construction firms, restaurants, and other businesses. But it was a false, ephemeral prosperity. Our city was rotting away with moral decay, and the situation was only growing worse every day.

At first people didn't seem to care. The prosperity seemed to blind them to the true condition of our city. But later it became a great and growing social concern. These men were ruling our city and we were going down quickly. Because officials could easily be bribed, not even the international drug agencies were able to catch the drug lords. It seemed that they always came close, but never quite managed to catch them.

By 1995 we had been living under these conditions for almost a decade. The Christian leadership began to realize that our city would be spiritually lost without drastic intervention. But at that time, evangelical Christians numbered only around 50,000, in a city of about two million people, and very few of the evangelicals were professionals. If all the experts and funds from the international drug enforcement agencies could not accomplish anything, how could we? What could a small, poor church do in the face of this desperate situation? Then again, we do have a God that can do anything.

At that time, two of the pastors in the city were preparing an all-night prayer meeting in the Coliseum. The Christian leadership responded to the call to prayer for our city. Maybe, just maybe, the Lord would do something—if we would call on His name together.

During the previous years the Ministers' Association held monthly, united meetings in different churches, but very few people attended besides those from the particular church where it was held. Nonetheless, the Association accepted the invitation to praise and pray together—for a whole night.

Little did we realize just what the Lord would do through that first united prayer meeting. Nor did we realize that it would be the first of many gatherings through which the Lord would work in our city to bring about the move of His Spirit.

The First Prayer *Vigilia*

So the time was set—March 1995—to pray all night in the Coliseum. It was planned for the Sunday night of a three-day weekend, so that people could rest on Monday. Pastors, leaders, and our congregations were invited. No one really expected much of a turnout, but at least we knew the church leadership would make an effort to be there. If even 2,000 people attended, we would have considered it a great success. Other than wanting to pray for a change in our society, we had no specific goal. There was no planned agenda.

To our amazement, 20,000 people showed up for the *vigilia!* It seems that the church at large understood that if God didn't intervene, we were lost. The night was filled with praise and worship and prayer. Since it was our first *vigilia* and we hadn't planned on so many people attending, it lacked adequate organization. An observer could easily have concluded, "This is a good idea; it might work some day. Just let me know when you get it better organized and I'll be back. In the meantime, I'll pack my bags."

We, too, could have focused on a thousand errors and gotten upset with the organization. But we knew that the Lord looked down from the heavenlies and was delighted to see His children gathered in one place, all getting along, and praising His name. Truly His ways are higher than our ways, and His thoughts are higher than our thoughts. We quickly learned that lesson.

We also discovered that *God answers prayer!* On that particular weekend, authorities would ordinarily expect dozens of murders, but the front-page story on Tuesday morning was this: *"No Murders over the Weekend!"*

Yes, the united prayer of the people of God had changed the statistics of the city! It is possible!

Then, just ten days later, there was another front-page story: the first drug lord had fallen! Some Christians actually read the paper and thought, "Well, it's about time, after all these years!"

No! It was the Lord answering the simple prayers of His children! Yes, we can change the history of our cities and nations! But first we need to learn to seek His face and pray together. We don't need expertise or funds; we need to seek the face of our Lord who is interested in the affairs of men and loves our cities.

This message resounded in our hearts and we wanted more, so we started plans for the next *vigilia*. The pastors decided that they would get the Coliseum again in August.

"No, no", said Julio. "Why should we get the Coliseum again when we already filled it? We need a larger place. We need to get the stadium."

There was a discussion about how we could possibly fill it and pay for it, but in the end it was clear that we needed to get the Pascual Guerrero Stadium for our August *vigilia*.

The March for Jesus in Our City

Meanwhile, in May 1995, the Ministers' Association participated for the first time in the International March for Jesus. The event drew about 30,000 believers. Among them were men and women of all ages, mothers carrying babies in their arms, small children and young people, and even some individuals in wheelchairs or on crutches. No one wanted to miss the event! For one-and-a-half hours, the city was paralyzed as we marched joyfully down the streets of Cali.

Students often hold protest marches in our city, receiving press coverage. Our March for Jesus, however, did not even get a brief mention in the newspapers. But we did not care. We weren't marching to be applauded by the public; we were satisfied to know that we were obeying the Lord and proclaiming our faith. We were more aware that the Lord had strategically placed us in our city to bring about a change and reverse the city's downward course.

Our First *Vigilia* in the Stadium

In August of 1995, we had our first *vigilia* in the stadium, with 40,000 Christians in attendance. The mayor, Mauricio Guzman and his wife, Luz Elena, were there to extend an official greeting. Just after the meeting began at around 9 p.m., there was an abrupt interruption: all the lights went out and we were plunged into darkness! It was a power failure, with no electricity available in the stadium to even address the crowd. Not even the emergency stand-by generators worked.

This was a very rare occurrence, indeed. Cali is the sports capital of Colombia, and the people are very enthusiastic fans.

They would not tolerate a power failure in any sports event. At any other time, there would have been total chaos under such circumstances. People would have stampeded, pushed, yelled and shoved each other. The angry mob would have trampled down the gates to get to the field, and some would have lost their lives in the melee. Far from being an exaggeration, this is the stark reality of life in Cali. But this night was different. The presence of God was there. We could feel it.

Without any prompting, people instinctively gathered together in small groups. Some began praying, others began praising God. Some ministered to those around them. People turned their eyes on Jesus and called on Him, praising and worshiping Him. It was a quiet, sacred place. The peace of God was present and was reflected through His people. As time went on, the atmosphere didn't change; it was a cathedral of praise. An intense and potentially dangerous situation had turned into an opportunity to minister to the Lord.

As the mayor and his wife watched this unusual phenomenon unfold, they had to have realized that these people, who call themselves Christians, were different from others in their city. This was no ordinary crowd of sports fans. Not only were they different, they had something that the mayor himself needed: the peace of God in the midst of turmoil. On that day, the mayor realized that these were people he hadn't known. A seed was planted in the mayor's heart, and he would remember this in the days to come.

After an hour-and-a-half the lights were restored and we began the service again. Following the mayor's greeting, the pastors asked him to declare Jesus as Lord over Cali. He proclaimed, "Cali belongs to Jesus Christ!" In one accord, thousands of believers jumped to their feet. The stands reverberated with applause. The people screamed with delight. Our highest city official had declared that Cali belonged to our Lord and Savior!

The pastors had anticipated that many people would be attending the *vigilia* out of curiosity. At night people leave the stadium after a soccer game. But on this occasion, tens of thousands of people were entering the stadium. Since there was no entrance fee, the curious had nothing to lose. With that expectation, the pastors had asked my husband Julio to preach an evangelistic message at midnight.

The visitors watched as we praised the Lord and prayed for our city. Then Julio preached the Word of God in power, and we witnessed many miraculous healings. The crippled got out of their wheelchairs or left their canes. A 13-year-old boy, a deaf mute since birth, heard for the first time! Coming up to the microphone, he said his first word, "Jesus!" And many more healings followed.

Then an even greater thing happened. When the invitation for salvation was given, between 4,000 and 5,000 people gave their lives to the Lord Jesus Christ! We realized that God was moving in a wonderful and powerful way. Truly the presence of God was there, permeating the entire place with His glory. It certainly wasn't the same as being in a stadium packed with people cheering for their team or for a concert of some popular singer. This was a holy place with the presence of the Lord! To me it was one of the most wonderful things I had ever experienced. I thought to myself, "Can there be anything more wonderful?" And just that moment the Holy Spirit spoke into my spirit, "This is not an end in itself; it is a means to an end." I sensed the Lord urging me on to something beyond what we were experiencing at that moment. The Lord was letting me know that this was not a place to camp but a means to move us toward what God had in store for us.

The Cost of Unity

...unless a grain of wheat falls into the ground and dies,
it remains alone; but if it dies, it produces much grain.

John 12:24, NKJV

It was November 1995 and time for our third *vigilia*. Only months had gone by since we had started praying together for our city as one body in the stadium. During these months the government, for no apparent reason, had come down hard on the cartel, and the police force had been purged. Six of the seven major drug lords had fallen; the seventh turned himself in nine months later. The public only knew that radical social changes were taking place. However, we knew that God had intervened because His people were praying together for our city. And the history of our city was beginning to change!

In this *vigilia* we held a candle-lighting ceremony. Alfonso Diaz, the president of the Ministers' Association at that time, asked everyone to bring a candle. Sometime after midnight, the stadium lights were turned off. Alfonso lit a torch and passed its flame to a few candles in one section of the first tier of the stadium. From there the flame went from one person to the next. This happened in each tier. Soon the entire stadium was ablaze with light. In this way, we were proclaiming that our source of light is Jesus alone, and that together we can become a light to the city.

We also distributed flyers listing the names and addresses of all the churches preaching sound doctrine, whether or not they took part in these prayer vigils. We wanted new converts to find a church close to their home so that they could become involved in church life throughout the week rather than just on Sundays. (The cost of transportation in Cali is a problem for people who already have a tight budget.) Slowly we were beginning to see a paradigm shift from being church-oriented to kingdom-oriented.

Death Threats

Alongside this move of God in our midst, a stream of death threats from our next-door neighbor, "Pepe," marked these months in 1995. Throughout the year the frequency and seriousness of the threats escalated. During the first months, Pepe had hired thieves to enter our property and steal money and other items from the offices. In the process, they shot one of our young people, Oscar, in the neck, and left a note on the school blackboard saying that they would return for Pastor Julio. (Miraculously, Oscar recovered without any permanent damage.)

As the year went on, Pepe's threats increased. At one point a deep, guttural voice, not his own, spoke out from him saying, "Why have you come to take our land?" We knew we weren't dealing with flesh and blood, but with demonic spirits.

Pepe was a neighbor who had already tried to steal some of our land by removing the barbed-wire fence that marked our northern boundary. He was accustomed to stealing land, using extortion and death threats to silence his victims. Most people were so intimidated that they withdrew their police charges against him.

Julio was uneasy about Pepe's constant threats. With hope that he could make peace with him, Julio went to Pepe's house to ask if he had offended him in some way. Pepe replied, "Don't listen to me; I am just a loud mouth." After shaking hands, Julio believed that things would surely change. However, within days Pepe resumed his threats.

Seeking the Lord's Perspective

Perplexed by this, Julio decided to fast and pray until the Lord gave him an understanding of what was happening. Three days into the fast, Julio had his answer. "The Lord told me that Pepe will do us great damage, but through it the move of God will come to Cali." We didn't give much thought to what the Lord meant by "damage." It didn't seem important in light of His promise for the city.

Because the Lord had already told Julio to get protection, we had hired a bodyguard, whom I will call Andres, who accompanied Julio everywhere he went. The threats continued, through telephone calls and letters. One day, hit men intercepted our car, warning us that they would kill Julio and Andres by the end of the year.

Pepe himself tried to gun down Andres, but the Lord miraculously spared his life—the three bullets missed him. We continued to take all the precautions we could, yet our faith rested ultimately in God's protection. Only He could save us. As Julio often remarked, "A presidential candidate with 14 bodyguards was killed; we know that our real protection comes from the Lord. I know that I am immortal until I have done all that the Lord has for me to do."

Fasting for Unity and the Move of God

It was December and elections were coming up for the Ministers' Association. Alfonso Diaz, an excellent leader, had been president. His spiritual maturity and experience had made him the right one for handling the pressures at this crucial time in Cali. He had remained humble despite the crowds coming to the *vigilias*, and he knew how to maintain balance. Prior to this year the low profile of the Ministers' Association made the presidency a position looked upon by many as time consuming and not worth the work involved. However, after three well-attended *vigilias*, a large March for Jesus, and an obvious move of God within Cali, the position looked a lot better. Whoever was elected president now would become more prominent in the public eye. Anyone seeking a name for himself would now find the position quite attractive. Julio was concerned at the possibility that churches might want to have their representative elected, rather than seeking the man of God for this important hour in the history of the city.

The importance of this hour weighed so heavily on Julio that he felt the need to fast and pray, asking the Lord to raise up the right leadership for the Ministers' Association, one who would be humble and able to promote unity. Julio knew that although our unity was so amazingly wonderful, it was also incredibly fragile.

During this time of fasting, we spent more hours than usual in prayer together. Julio travailed in spirit for two specific areas. First, he prayed that unity in the body of Christ would continue to deepen and grow in Cali. Secondly, he prayed for the move of God in this city, sensing that it was imminent. He labored in prayer that others would understand the importance of the hour as well.

The Final Exam

During that month our understanding of unity was challenged. At issue was a small Christian television station. The Lord had provided us with a small transmitter, antenna, tower, and basic equipment for production. The government, which had owned all the stations, announced that they would allow privately owned stations. Since the legislation did not yet specify how to obtain a permit, we were able to get on the air temporarily as a community station. Since we were still learning about production and needed more equipment, our programming was limited to showing the Jesus film at certain hours every day.

Julio kept trying, unsuccessfully, to get the pastors in Cali interested. He reported every little bit of progress at meetings of the Ministers' Association, hoping that someone would catch the vision for Christian television. But Colombia had been so tightly closed to evangelical Christianity, it was inconceivable to the pastors that Christian television could work. It seemed like a nice dream, but impossible. At times, this discouraged Julio.

Then one day, to our surprise, Julio received a fax from the group that had given us the transmitter and antenna. They asked us why we were not sharing the television with other pastors. Shocked at this accusation, Julio called the donors to find out what was going on. He was told that Pastor Roberto had complained to them.

At this Julio was upset, especially in light of our reconciliation with Roberto and what the Lord was working through the unity of the pastors in Cali. "How can this be? How can Roberto be doing this after all the Lord has done?" Vexed in his spirit, Julio finally told me, "I'm just going to make an appointment and confront Roberto with the situation. We can't be going through this at this stage."

However, he delayed in making an appointment with Roberto and remained disturbed in his spirit. It was beyond his understanding how something like this could happen.

Several days later, Julio asked me, "Honey, why is this happening?" Without thinking, I blurted out, "It's your final exam. This has nothing to do with Roberto. God is putting you through a final exam to see how much you really believe in unity.

"If Roberto has done wrong," I continued, "God will deal with him and help him see his error. But the question now is, will you allow this to offend you? It is like Joseph and his brothers. They sold him into slavery, and later Joseph gave them another opportunity, this time to legitimately sell the father's favorite son, Benjamin. But because they had repented, they did not sell him. This later resulted in their salvation.

"Now God is giving you a final exam. Will you be offended?" I asked.

To that he exclaimed, "Yes, that is it!" And he went to make an appointment with Roberto and his wife.

The following day, December 11, four days into our fast, Roberto and his wife were sitting in our home and being treated royally. Julio never even mentioned the problem, but wholeheartedly extended himself to them in a way that left me astonished. At one point, when Julio had to go upstairs for something, Roberto turned to me and asked, "Do you get many people attending your church as a result of your television programs?" When I explained that we had no way of knowing, since we only ran the Jesus film, and the name of our church did not appear anywhere on the screen, he seemed surprised. "Oh, I thought you were showing your own programs," he said.

When Julio came back to the room, he and Roberto finished talking and then prayed together. After Roberto and his wife left, Julio asked me, "How did I do?"

"You acted as the holy man of God that you are. I am proud of you," I replied.

It was not until a few days later that I fully understood why I had used the words "final exam" instead of "testing". It truly was a final exam that Julio needed to pass in order to qualify for what awaited him on December 13.

The Cost to Be Paid

It was now the sixth day of his fast and Julio was excited about going to the board meeting of the Ministers' Association. He left for the meeting at the Presbyterian church with great enthusiasm. He was convinced that the Lord had heard his prayers and was going to move in a powerful way, far beyond anything we could ever imagine. As a result, we would see the history of our city and nation changed! Yes, we stood at the threshold of receiving these promises!

A few minutes after he left, I received a telephone call from one of the pastors, who told me that Julio had just been shot. When I arrived at the church, Julio's body was lying on the sidewalk at the entrance to the church's property. He had been shot by assassins who had waited for him in ambush.

As I got out of the car, the Lord spoke to my spirit: "Precious in the sight of the LORD is the death of his saints" (Psalm 116:15), and I knew I was on holy ground. The blood of a true martyr was shed there. I sat down on the sidewalk next to my husband.

At that moment, unable even to pray, I began calling on the name of our Lord Jesus Christ. Then I knew that I had to settle it immediately with the Lord (and in reality for myself). It was a prayer that I needed to say out loud:

Lord, I know you are perfect and do all things well. You would never do anything to compromise Your plan or to hurt me; therefore, I accept this, too, from Your hand and I want You to know that it is well with my soul.

Looking back, I believe it was the Lord Himself who put that prayer in my heart when I called on His name. This horrible tragedy was also, amazingly, profoundly sacred.

The entire city of Cali was moved by Julio's death. The newspapers, television stations, and radio programs all carried reports for days. One article was entitled, "They Killed the Last Living Saint!" In the soccer stadium, during the half-time ceremonies in the final game of a series, a minute of silence took place in his honor. Brethren from Brazil told us that the porters in the airport were discussing Julio's death, as did the taxi driver on their way into town.

Even a drug lord contacted us, offering his bodyguards, bullet-proof cars, or anything else that we might need. Of course, we did not accept the offer. He then acknowledged needing what we have, and asked us to help them! Even guerrilla fighters came and stood on the mountain behind our church property, waving white flags!

A Historical Event: A Covenant of Unity

Julio's funeral service was held at our church on December 16, 1995. The church overflowed with people representing many different cities in Colombia, as well as five other nations. Two Indian tribes were represented as well. Priests and nuns were there.

The three largest sympathy bouquets came from an unusual assortment of Christians: the Baptist seminary, a large charismatic church, and nuns from a near-by school. Many people gave personal testimony to the impact of Julio's life. I received messages from people in 20 countries. The two most common sentences were: "He was a father to me," and, "I only met him once, but my life was totally changed."

The Lord gave our family incredible strength as we shared publicly our absolute belief that Julio's martyrdom was a seed that would produce a harvest far beyond what we could now understand. It was a message of challenge to seek the Lord and to continue in His strength, to see His plan come forth in fullness.

Toward the end of the service, Alfonso Diaz, the president of the Ministers' Association, asked me if the pastors could join together to make a covenant of unity before the Lord. The idea was to promise God, and each other, that we would work together in unity to see His purposes fulfilled in our land and that nothing would be allowed to separate us—that we were one. Of course, I gave my consent and we embraced one another, making that covenant.

The presence of the Lord was so real that everyone could sense it. I believe that it was at this moment that we stepped from cooperation into unity.

For me, this was one of the most important events in the history of Cali. In spite of our deep sorrow, there was also joy as we waited expectantly for what the Lord would do next. When there is sacrifice, God sends the fire. If united prayer had caused the drug cartel to collapse, strongholds to be pulled down, and the gospel to go forward, imagine how much more could be achieved through the blood of a martyr!

Serious Consideration

Within two months of Julio's death, the pastors in Cali went through more shaking. Two pastors died, both around 40 years of age. These deaths, although caused by illnesses, spoke clearly into the hearts of the leaders about the shortness of life. When confronted with the deaths of those who are active in ministry and in the prime of life, we think more seriously about our priorities and what the Lord is saying to us. This brought many pastors into a more serious place of walking in unity.

Unity, a Key Word

When the elections for the Ministers' Association took place, Alfonso Diaz was re-elected, and I was invited to participate on the board of directors to honor Julio. In these meetings, I witnessed the godly resolution of countless problems between churches and pastors. "Unity" was a key word. These men of God on the board frequently reminded each other of the covenant that they had made. They worked into the night to seek the mind of the Lord for the answers to vexing problems. More mature leaders would take a loss before letting a younger man become offended. There was a deliberate choice of unity.

What Will It Take?

Frequently, the question is raised in Christian circles, what will it take to cause us to walk in unity? There seems to be a common factor: desperation. Until we get to a place where we are desperate to see the Lord move in our midst, nothing seems to happen. The question that follows is, how do we get desperate? I believe there are two paths to desperation. The first is persecution or some form of intense pressure. The other is spiritual passion—for the heart of the Lord.

Pressure from outside sources seems to make us forget the non-essentials and put our priorities in order. It was the difficult situation in Cali that made us start to seek the Lord in a fresh way.

However, a higher path is to have the passion of the heart of the Lord for our cities and nations, without having to go through pressures or persecution. John Knox is well remembered for his words, *"Give me Scotland, or I die!"* Only a man with the vision and passion of Jesus can pray a prayer like that. When we spend time with the Lord and intercede for our cities and nations, we begin to see them in a different light. Instead of seeing the sin, violence, decadence, and such, we begin to see what the Lord intended that city to be; we see the calling that God has for that place. Then we can no longer be satisfied with things as they are. The only thing that will satisfy us is seeing our city respond to the call of God, and His call causes us to intercede more fervently and to walk with those who have the same vision.

All we need to do is to lay aside our schedules, agendas, burdens, and cares, and take on God's. Unity will always call for some form of death—probably not as martyrs—but certainly death to our own dreams and desires, so that the Lord's desires may come forth. At the same time, we realize that His yoke is easy and His burden is light. As we begin to walk with Him in believing for our communities, we find that He is there to answer.

First Steps in Unity

*For there the Lord commanded
the blessing—life forevermore.*
Psalm 133:3b, NKJV

As we began walking in this new unity, we realized that Cali had no specific apostolic leader. However, we had many fine leaders who, working together with the covenant of unity, could accomplish the purposes of God. As we have already seen in our discussion of Genesis 11, with unity "nothing...will be impossible to them."

The next *vigilia* was scheduled for Holy Thursday, the day before Good Friday, in 1996. The crowds thronged the stadium. People had rented buses to come from the surrounding areas. Even representatives from the Guambiano and Paez tribes participated in what the Lord was doing in our city. The stadium was packed with about 50,000 people. Even the *vigilia* itself seemed to have matured. Prayer had taken on a new depth that we hadn't experienced previously. In August, the last major drug lord would turn himself in to the authorities. God was definitely doing a new thing in our city.

A Special Request from the Mayor

Later that year, a few months before Christmas, a commission from the mayor's office arrived at one of the local churches. They were planning activities for the *Feria*, a traditional Christmas celebration in Cali noted for its debauchery. Some consider it to be like the Mardi Gras in New Orleans or the Carnival in Rio de Janeiro. During these celebrations many churches plan to go away for a retreat or camp meetings. This year the mayor's office approached an evangelical church to ask them to participate, bringing Christian music and the Christian message to the festivities. The invitation came from the same mayor who had attended the first *vigilia* in the stadium, and now wanted the Christians to share their message—with all the expenses paid. The local church that received the invitation very kindly told the commission that they would be unable to participate as a local church, but would be very happy to participate if the invitation were extended to the whole Christian church in Cali.

Some days later, the commission took the same invitation to the Ministers' Association, which received it gladly. To this day very few people even know that the invitation was first given to a local church; they were never told. No one wanted the glory to go anywhere except to our Lord Jesus Christ.

That Christmas *Feria*, for the first time in the history of Cali, brought the gospel message to crowds of people who had come with a very different agenda. The whole atmosphere of the Feria changed. Wild partying was mixed with a message of truth and seriousness.

Some were pleased and found the Lord; others were disappointed. Some Christians were disappointed, too. They felt that the church's presentation at the *Feria* was too ingrown and not adequately directed toward the type of people attending the event. I'm sure we could have done better, but the church lacked experience and was still learning how to reach the world in its own setting. We were too used to evangelistic crusades and other methods that are commonly taught in our churches. We weren't comfortable in a situation like the *Feria*, but we were learning. The important thing is that the Lord's name was glorified and many did come to know the Lord as their Savior.

The Gospel Penetrating Society

At the end of the year, new elections were held for the Ministers' Association. Roosevelt Muriel was elected president and served for a two-year term (1997–1998). He had been active on the board of directors and understood well what the Lord was doing in our midst.

As the Lord began moving in the city church, the Association changed as well. It could no longer be contained in a box of files, or maintained with a few meetings. Given the new needs, Roosevelt was the man of God's choosing. During this time, the Presbyterians and Baptists began participating more fully in the city church, adding a broader dimension and great strength to the work.

At the same time, the gospel was starting to reach into new areas of society. Persons from a higher socio-economic level had come to know the Lord, along with prominent members of society: sports commentators, businessmen, lawyers, news reporters, professional athletes, and the like. And they were not ashamed to share their testimony with others. Previously, evangelical Christianity was considered a religion for the uneducated people, but now the gospel was reaching into all areas of society.

Holy Thursday's *Vigilia* 1998

The *vigilia* on Holy Thursday 1998 was awesome. One section of the stadium was being repaired, limiting capacity to about 45,000. Another 15,000 people stood outside waiting, hoping that someone would leave so that they could enter. People came not only from Cali, but also from the surrounding areas and other cities and countries. The police, who came to control the crowd, found that the people outside had started a prayer walk for the *vigilia* inside. They waited throughout the night, making their way into the stadium one or two at a time as others eventually left. The presence of the Lord was powerful that night as God's people met in unity to seek His face. There was a fresh atmosphere, a deepened repentance for personal sin and the sins of our city. There was a definite step forward in maturity.

A Christian Television Station in Cali

In the meantime, our church was struggling again with the issue of television. Single-handedly, Julio had managed to get the station on the air. Although the pastors had been skeptical to the idea of Christian television at first, some later caught the vision. Among these was Roosevelt Muriel, the new president of the Ministers' Association. Roosevelt excels in encouraging and helping others to believe in the visions and promises of God, making them become a reality. So in 1998, we turned the television station over to the Ministers' Association, which named the station *TeleUnidad* (Tele Unity).

Roosevelt and a well-chosen team began running with the vision. We had fund-raising dinners and were constantly in prayer for the project. If there was ever a time when something could be done with this important media, it was now; but it would take unity among the churches and pastors to handle such a huge project. Since the Lord had been calling professionals to Himself, we had people of expertise and experience that joined in the vision. It took us more than a year to put the vision on paper and to prepare the television project for the National Commission of Colombian Television under the Ministry of Communications, and then more time for them to review it.

In the spring of 1999, the Ministers' Association asked me to go with Roosevelt and a Christian layman working on the project to Bogota, to receive the papers for *TeleUnidad*—the first private

Christian station ever approved by the government. In fact, it is rare for a national government to give a television license to a ministerial association.

The government was so impressed with the project proposal that they sent other institutions to us for advice in writing up their projects. God was lifting up His church to be a blessing to others. It was possible because God had brought professional people to the foot of the cross; when they met Jesus, they brought their knowledge to the cross as well.

It took us another year and a half of tremendous work trying to raise funds just for the most basic equipment. We didn't even have half of what was necessary, but by renting a small transmitter, we made the deadline of August 15, 2000 and went on air. For the first time in the history of Colombia, evangelical Christians had a television station. Even as I write this book, we feel like we are chopping down a forest with a razor blade, but the Lord has been faithful and we know He will see us through.

Church Growth with Participation in City Events

God continued to do incredible things in our city. In one year the number of churches increased by 50 percent, from 214 churches in early 1998 to more than 300. The local churches also reported numerical growth. A city-church evangelism outreach, dividing the city into 24 sections with simultaneous crusades, brought many into the kingdom of God.

The city government initiated a pro-family moralization project called *"Cali sos vos"* ("You are Cali") and asked Christians to manage it. The mayor's office granted the stadium for the *vigilia* without charging us rent. God was working in the most incredible ways.

In the meantime, the Ministers' Association had grown in every respect. It was during Roosevelt's term that we rented offices and began hiring personnel. We walked through the Association's expanding role in the city step by step until everyone was comfortable with the change.

When Roosevelt became president, no one was really prepared for all that would be involved. The position became very demanding on his time, and as a result his church suffered. By God's grace and strength they pulled through, but it wasn't easy. In the process, we learned to stand together with them. By the time of the next elections, we were better prepared.

A Voice in Society

Before Julian Collazos became a candidate, the church board and congregation were asked to count the cost of having to share their pastor with the city-church. It would be two years of arduous work and they needed to prepare for it. They prayed and believed that, should their pastor be elected, God would give them the grace to step up to the challenge. Julian was elected president of the Association for the 1999–2000 term. His gifts were needed for the steps we were taking as a united church. During these last two administrations, the Lord had been working to bring us to maturity as a city church.

When the Cali cartel was active, the drug lords invested much of their profits in the city. Businesses prospered and there was much construction throughout the city. With the fall of the cartel, our whole economic system was shaken. As a result, we were thrown into the worst recession in the history of the country, at least since 1905, when records began being kept. Unemployment soared to 19.7 percent and the people of Cali, noted for their happy spirit, were discouraged. The change was so obvious that the mayor became concerned and announced a week of celebration called "*Promotora de la Paz*" ("Promoter of Peace") in March 2000. He invited the city's churches to participate in the activities.

One of the most prestigious meetings involved the participation of those considered by the mayor to be the three most influential persons in our society. The mayor invited them to speak about the problems in the city and to encourage the people. The first two speakers were the governor of our state and the archbishop of the

Roman Catholic Church. They expressed their concern for the city and their appreciation for its people, who were passing through trying and difficult times; they were standing with us. The third person to speak was Julian Collazos, President of the Ministers' Association. He spoke about God's love and concern for the people and gave the city a message of hope in Jesus. Immediately after the meeting the governor went directly to Julian saying, "That is the message that we need to hear."

Just a few years before, the evangelical church was not considered important enough to have a message pertinent to the people of our city. God had changed the way that society was seeing the church of Jesus Christ. This may be common in the United States, where the voice of the Christians has long been heard and respected, but for us it was an incredible change that only the Lord could bring about.

Congress on Unity

Early in 1999 the Lord started stirring Roosevelt with the idea that we should hold a Congress on Unity for other nations, so that they could see what the Lord was doing in Cali. The news had begun to spread and brethren from other countries had started to visit our city. Roosevelt presented his idea to the Association, and it was felt that this was from the Lord for the city church. The congress was scheduled for August, which did not leave us much time for organizing such a large event.

Our desire was to make the congress available to as many Christian leaders as possible. But we quickly recognized a major problem: finances. Travel in South America is very expensive. Registration for a four-day event of this sort normally costs about $150—a month's salary for many people in our region. Then there are hotel expenses, food, and local transportation. Such expenses would exclude far too many people we wanted to be there. Our desire was to make the congress available to anyone who really wanted to come.

It was wonderful to see how the Lord directed our steps. First of all, we decided to charge only $20 for the congress. We realized this would not cover our expenses, but felt it was what the Lord was asking us to do. In addition to the registration fee, each participant would also have to arrange for his own travel to the event.

The Ministers' Association appointed an inter-church protocol committee to organize the event. Through the work of this committee, Christian families opened their homes, offering bed or meals or both. Local churches made rooms available for sleeping quarters. People with cars offered transportation for the duration of the congress. Others served as translators. We offered the congress in English, French, and German, all at no charge to the participant. We had a selection of 16 morning and afternoon sessions with top speakers. At night we had united meetings in a coliseum.

The congress measured up to the best of any large conference in the United States that I have ever seen. It was a city-church effort and everyone gave his best. No one was interested in inquiring about what church an individual came from; we honestly didn't care.

For There the Lord Commands Blessing and Salvation

On the last night of the congress we had a *vigilia* in the stadium. Because of the schedule, it was not an all-night meeting, but it went on till midnight. We had an excellent evangelist there from the United States. Many people were miraculously healed. I particularly remember an infant whose skin was filled with sores from having been born to a mother with syphilis. The baby was healed and had perfectly healthy skin within minutes.

At the invitation, about 5,000 came to the Lord. People streamed down from the second and third tiers of the stadium, making their way to the bleachers on the ground level. Seekers from all three levels joined together on the track, praying the sinner's prayer. It was like a waterfall of people cascading to Jesus' feet. Again we were seeing salvation come to our city. The visitors to the Congress of Unity were overwhelmed. Most of them had never seen anything like it before.

Toward the end of the meeting, Roosevelt was walking on the track and met a man from the mayor's office. The man, obviously moved by the event, commented to him, "I have never seen anything like this." Roosevelt put his hand on the man's chest and said, "The only thing lacking is that you give your life to Jesus Christ." With that the man began to cry and Roosevelt had the privilege of leading him to the Lord.

The next morning we had a breakfast for all the visiting pastors. They were given an opportunity to share their thoughts. All of them repeated the same idea in different words: "We have never seen anything like this. It wasn't just a conference with information. The love and working together in unity is like a dream that we didn't think we would ever see. The Lord is here." A group of pastors from Texas added, "Our prayer is that we will be able to take even a small coal from this fire back to our city." It was truly a wonderful and awesome experience.

Diversity in Unity

The body is a unit, though it is made up of many parts;
and though all its parts are many, they form one body.
1 Corinthians 12:12 a

During these last five years, we have learned a lot about what unity is—and what it isn't. In Ephesians 4, Paul speaks of unity of the Spirit and unity of the faith. When I speak of unity, I am referring to the former. Unity of the faith is an outcome of unity of the Spirit; it is not something we should pursue, lest we fall into the temptation of wanting everyone else to think as we do. This would be foolish since none of us has the whole truth, but rather portions of the truth. Unity of the faith will be complete when Jesus comes and we all see eye to eye. In the meantime, we can have, and are told to pursue, unity of the Spirit.

We have already seen that unity is not merely cooperation, although that is a first step. Neither is it uniformity, as each person needs to reflect the Lord according to the capacity and unique calling that he has been given. Nor is it unanimity; not everyone has to participate in or be in agreement with absolutely everything that is done. There is always diversity in unity, a diversity that we learn to appreciate more every day.

Allow for Diversity

As we began walking together in unity, different pastors shared what the Lord seemed to be speaking into their hearts about the city. I remember one day at a board of directors' meeting when the pastor of a large church presented what the Lord was saying to him: "I believe God wants us to anoint the city with oil!"

The obvious question was, "How do we do that?"

He immediately replied, "We will sprinkle it with oil from a helicopter. Our church will pay for it."

Right away, you could sense that some pastors felt this suggestion was a bit out of line. Yet we had discovered that the Lord has a different calling for each pastor and church. Those who felt led to do this joined the pastor who had proposed the idea. The other pastors, even though they did not participate, supported them, saying, "Our church does not feel led to take part in this but if you feel the Lord is telling you to do this, then you should go ahead. We won't stand in your way, nor will we talk against you. We will support you and pray for you as you carry it out."

And so we anointed the city with oil. We might ask, did it do any good? We cannot measure the effect that something like this has on a city, but we do know that being obedient to the prompting of the Holy Spirit is always right; God will take care of the rest.

Not long afterwards another pastor felt that we should march around the city as the Israelites had done around Jericho. Not all the churches participated, but once again, they didn't oppose it either.

We hired buses to leave from four strategic locations in the city—north, west, south, and east. Because of rush-hour traffic problems, the city would only grant us a permit for four o'clock in the morning. From all parts of Cali, Christians went to the nearest pick-up point to get on a bus and ride around the city, praying as they went. The last day of this Jericho march had been scheduled for Monday, a holiday. That day, all the buses ended up at the coliseum where we met together for a time of prayer and praise. It was a wonderful day.

Those who took part didn't hold an "attitude" towards those who did not take part, or vice versa. We had learned that each of us has a different calling from the Lord and we need to work according to the specific leading He gives us. Whether or not we take part in these activities does not make us any more or less "spiritual"—it makes us obedient to His leading for us.

Serving Our City

In Cali, the Lord has raised up Christian professionals who have been able to participate in government affairs. Some have stepped into positions in the city government. Others have become members of the Peace Commission, handling the delicate situations between the government and guerrilla forces. Obviously, not everyone can work at this level, but we all have opportunities in one way or another to serve, according to the capacity that the Lord has given us.

The Ministers' Association once asked the mayor how the church might help serve our city. One problem was with garbage collection in a certain area of the city, so we offered our help. In coordination with the city government, 1,500 believers gathered on a Saturday morning to collect garbage—40 tons of it. In the process 500 people came to know the Lord as their Savior! We didn't realize that it would be a city-church evangelistic garbage team! We discovered that service opens doors in a wonderful way to win people to Jesus.

Worship Teams

One of the first ways our congregations began working together was through worship teams. Originally, worship teams from different churches would participate in the all-night *vigilias*. Soon afterward, we started another worship team made up of musicians from different churches. This has been a great blessing. The musicians have been strengthened as they minister together, and the church can appreciate the talent that the Lord had given us in the united body.

Youth Ministry

With the new move of the Spirit, we formed a citywide youth group, creating new opportunities for fellowship, worship, evangelism, and service for church-based youth ministries. To make this possible, a youth minister was appointed by the Ministers' Association, and the youth from different churches made up the leadership team. They have had wonderful and refreshing experiences through camps, evangelistic outreaches, and various gatherings.

Perhaps it has been easier for the youth to find unity, because they don't come with the preconceived ideas and fears that many adults have. This group has been of great encouragement to the youth of our own church. Although the youth love walking together in unity, they also know where God has placed them; we haven't found them changing churches. Later we were also able to form an interchurch children's group.

Jesus en Las Calles

"Jesus in the Streets" is an evangelistic team that originally started in a local church. Now it has members from many churches. They are called to evangelism, but they also help in other ways. Of those contacted through their door-to-door evangelism, 80 percent have come to the Lord.

Grupo Uno

"Group One" was originally formed to help with the logistics of our *vigilias*. Now composed of about 800 people, mostly men, its purpose is to serve the body of Christ almost like a group of city deacons. Besides serving as ushers at the *vigilias*, they also help with evangelistic outreaches and numerous Christian events.

Mil Trompetas

Most of the churches have established intercession groups, but as a city-church we have formed *Mil Trompetas* (1,000 Trumpets), an interchurch intercessory group comprised of three or four of the main intercessors from different churches. The goal is to have 1,000 city-church intercessors. This group meets every Saturday morning to intercede for Cali and Colombia. During the week they break up into smaller groups and pray at strategic locations throughout the city.

My own approach to spiritual warfare is different from that of *Mil Trompetas*, but we don't allow that to become a problem. Intercessors from my church understand what we believe, but we don't need to discuss that with the city-church intercessors. These are non-essential matters that would only bring discord, something that the enemy would like very much—keeping the brethren from praying together. As we continue to pray with one another, we learn from one another, resulting in spiritual growth and greater compatibility.

Standing Together

The pastors on the board of the Ministers' Association are not perfect; the Lord is still working on areas in our lives. Yet these are mighty men and women of God, and they are being used to fulfill His purposes at this crucial hour in the history of our city and nation. One has to choose what to see: the problems that arise from time to time, or the Lord at work bringing us to greater maturity. The former divides; the latter promotes unity. And as we work through different problems, solutions are found at the foot of the cross.

The most difficult situations are those involving immorality in the leadership. When these have arisen, the city pastors have been there to help with the restoration of the fallen leader and to stand with the hurting church. In one case, we were able to open the doors for a brother to go to Spain for his restoration. Through this difficult time, pastors from the city stepped in to help nurture and strengthen the congregation. This is one area that has moved my heart the most because it is so Christ-like.

We have learned that we must stand on the truth. It hasn't been easy to confront a brother who is from another denomination and could easily reject us. There is great risk of loss. But we have learned that when we stand on God's truth, we are also standing on the Rock, Jesus, who is the Truth. Walking together in unity has enabled us to go through some very difficult times together, and to see the Lord's victory when it seemed impossible.

In these last years, I have ministered extensively outside Colombia. When I am away, the pastors always offer to help our church by preaching, teaching, praying, or in any other possible way. When they preach, they minister the Word according to the need of our church, rather than sharing their own personal views.

The pastors have stood with us in difficult times. Since my husband's death, Pepe, the same man who threatened my husband's life, has also threatened my life and the lives of other leaders in our church. History has taught us that these are not idle threats. So pastors from the city have come to our property to pray with us. We are one. What happens in one church happens to us all. By the same token, as we have stood together, we have seen great victories.

If One Part is Honored...

Because of the price that our family has paid with the death of my husband, I feel that I have unity running through my veins. However, all too often the Lord has to show me just how much more I have to learn.

One day a pastor, a friend for many years, called to tell me about what the Lord was doing for him. For several years, he and his congregation had been praying for the opportunity to buy the houses on the block where their church is located in order to expand their work, but the owners had sworn they would never sell. That Sunday the pastor was thrilled to tell his congregation that one of the houses was for sale. He encouraged them to pray for the funds to buy it. One of the men of the church asked him how much was needed. It would be $100,000, a large sum for any church. Then the brother wrote a check for that sum and handed it to his pastor. It was an incredible, instant answer to prayer!

When I heard the pastor tell me the story, my first thought was, "I would love to have someone like that in my church!" But immediately the Holy Spirit spoke to my heart: "What would your reaction have been if it had been one of your daughters who had received $100,000?"

"I would be very happy for her," I replied.

"Exactly," the Holy Spirit continued. "And what is the difference between her and your brother? It is My church and it is all one. What happened to him happened to you too."

I felt about two inches high. I was ashamed to find myself still within the four walls of my church, rather than in the kingdom of God. Of course, the church is the Lord's, and we should rejoice with those who rejoice and weep with those who weep. Right then I began praying. First, I repented of my initial thought. Then I began interceding for that pastor and his church. I thanked the Lord for His provision and asked Him to multiply it and make it $200,000. I claimed all the houses on the block for that church! That week I think I prayed more for his church than mine. I truly wanted the Lord to *bless his ministry*.

Pray Rather Than Criticize

In Cali we have so many new converts that most of our churches find it difficult to disciple them adequately. Since I believe so strongly in discipleship, this has always been of great concern to me. I learned one day that one of our large, rapidly growing churches was forming new cell groups in the homes of brand new believers, and many of these groups were led by young people who were not spiritually mature believers.

Of course, this was of great concern to me. Here was a church whose pastor had also told his people he did not want them to call him "pastor" since Jesus was their only pastor. I think it was his way of trying to get them to focus their eyes on the Lord. But under those circumstances, how would the new believers in this church ever be properly discipled?

Right there I had a choice to make. Either I could let myself get upset over the problem, which would lead to criticism and disunity, or I could intercede for them. I chose the latter and began praying.

One of the first things the Holy Spirit spoke to my heart was that this pastor had the call of an evangelist! Suddenly it made sense to me. Of course, he didn't like to be called pastor. He was an evangelist. Perhaps he himself did not understand why he disliked being called pastor, but it had to do with his calling. That also explained why so many people were coming to the Lord through his ministry.

With this new insight, I began praying that the Lord would help him with the discipling of these new converts. I prayed that mature leaders, with a heart for pastoring, discipleship, and establishing of new believers, would support the cell groups and pastor.

Shortly afterwards, this pastor's radio station called me. Their programmer asked me to broadcast a program at prime time. Knowing we did not have the funds to pay for such a program, I thanked him but declined.

"You don't understand," the man explained. "We are offering you a program on our station free of charge."

"I'll pray about it and get back to you," I told him. But as time passed and I became involved in other activities, I forgot to even pray about it.

About a month later the programmer called me again, and once again I delayed my answer, wanting to pray about it.

A week or so later, I was in the pastor's office with some of the leaders of the Ministers' Association, and the pastor of this church publicly invited me to broadcast a program. Roosevelt Muriel, our

Association president, immediately spoke up, "Ruth, you need to take this program. You can at least use it for our Ministers' Association to encourage believers to pray." When I heard this and saw that others agreed, I understood it to be a confirmation from the Lord.

As soon as I began preparing for the program, the Lord opened my eyes. "You were praying for the new believers to be discipled, weren't you? Who do you think listens to this radio station? Isn't it the new believers? I want you to help disciple them."

I was stunned! Suddenly it all fit together. Had I not prayed for this pastor and his growing congregation, I don't believe the program would ever have been offered to me.

It is so easy to criticize others, yet it only breeds discontent and disunity. We can do so much more through prayer. Although it takes time, praying through a situation like this reveals to us another side of the issue that we could not see with our natural eyes.

Part II
Ingredients for
UNITY

Get God's Perspective

We must learn to judge our circumstances by who God is,
and not judge God by our circumstances.

Over the years, I have learned the importance of understanding that God's ways and thoughts are so much higher than ours (Isaiah 55:8–9). We need the mind of Christ to see circumstances from His perspective. Without this, we expect too little and are satisfied with so much less than His abundant plans for us.

My husband's death was the greatest tragedy I have ever experienced. Julio was so much more than an excellent husband and father. He was my best friend, counselor, and companion. We shared so much together. We had worked closely together to found and pastor two churches. We were living in a country that was not ours by birth. Those who knew us saw our marriage as ideal. It has not been easy for me to be a widow, nor has it been easy for my girls to be without a father—especially after having someone like him.

Yet in a tragedy like this, or any difficult situation in our lives, we must choose to believe in the sovereignty of God. My family and I can look at this tragedy from two perspectives. We must choose one.

On the one hand, we could choose to see Julio's death as the result of living in a violent city. We could focus on the injustice of a man being killed in the prime of life and ministry, especially when he was serving the Lord. However, if we choose this view, we will fall into bitterness and self-pity; without realizing it, we will also accuse God of being unjust and unfair, for He rules over all things.

The alternative is to see Julio's death as something permitted by the Lord in answer to our prayers for the city. This allows us to understand that God will use this situation to quicken His plan and purpose. It also allows us to see the sovereignty of our Lord, who lovingly walks with us and comforts us as we pass through a tragedy He has allowed for a higher purpose. In choosing this interpretation, we become God's instruments for sharing with others, especially those in need, that same comfort He has given to us. In this way, we strengthen the church. How important it is to judge our circumstances by who God is, and not judge God by our circumstances.

Competition or Expansion?

As I mentioned before, our Ministers' Association has its own television station, *TeleUnidad*. It was a long, difficult struggle for us just to get on the air, and we still need equipment and technology. It has been a gigantic project, and we count on everyone to do his share.

As we approached the government's deadline to get on the air, another pastor in Cali announced that he was going to start his own television station. You can imagine how disheartened we felt. We had been working so hard to get *TeleUnidad* going! Roosevelt, who had been heading up this television project, commented sadly, "This brother has become very marginal in the Ministers' Association." I understood the disappointment in his voice. I felt it myself.

The next day one of the pastors called Roosevelt with a suggestion: "I believe the Lord has spoken to me about this. Why don't we call this pastor and offer to help him get his television license. It just might be that the Lord is telling us that the move of

God is going to be so great in Cali that we will need two Christian television stations. If this is not of God, then things won't work out. The Lord will deal with this man in His own way."

I don't know if that message was relayed to the pastor or not. But since then, this pastor has quietly dropped all plans for a second television station and has now become more involved in our Ministers' Association.

Only time will reveal the purposes of God in human affairs. As we wait for this revelation, we need to be open to God's sovereign ways. So often He works in a manner we don't understand. Then when He acts, we are all too quick to give our own opinions before waiting to hear from Him. We need to learn to step back and allow God to do what He wants, in the way He wants.

When the Unexpected Happens

Too often we are like the two heartbroken disciples walking on the Emmaus road, who did not recognize the risen Christ walking beside them. It seemed as though the enemy had triumphed. It was the third day after the crucifixion and they did not recognize the Stranger who walked with them. Did they not recall what Jesus had told them would happen on the third day?

How like those disciples are we. We are so slow to understand the ways of the Lord. How we praise the Lord now for His death and for that precious third day when He arose! But at the time, it was another story—until all the pieces were put together and salvation came. When the unexpected happens, will we also become discouraged as the disciples were on the road to Emmaus? Will we lose faith?

Peter tells us that in the last days people will scoff and mock, questioning the Lord's Second Coming and saying that everything continues the same as from the beginning. If Jesus doesn't come exactly according to our eschatological framework, or if things today don't go the way we had planned, will our faith be shaken? Could that be why Jesus asks if He will find faith on earth upon His return?

Recognizing God's Answer to Our Prayers

Many times we pray for something and don't recognize that God has answered our prayer. Elijah prayed that it would not rain, and it did not rain for three years (1 Kings 17 and 18). The Lord sent him to the Brook Cherith, where he had water to drink, and the ravens brought him bread and meat each morning and evening. God provided wonderfully for the faithful prophet! However, as time went by, the brook dried up, for there had been no rain to sustain the brook. It was actually an answer to Elijah's prayer. So the Lord sent him to Zarephath, where a widow provided him with food.

Many times, when we see "our river" dry up, we don't recognize it as an answer to prayer. Likewise, when praying for our city, God sometimes does not answer us in the ways we expect Him to; in fact, outward circumstances often became far worse than before! If we don't recognize the hand of the Lord in the midst of our circumstances, we can easily become discouraged.

In Cali and Colombia, it is because the Lord is answering our prayers that we are going through difficult times. Several examples make this clear:

We prayed for the downfall of the drug cartel—and we were plunged into the worst recession ever recorded in Colombia's history. Unemployment soared to almost 20 percent! We are still in the midst of this severe recession, the worst in our history. God did answer our prayer. We are in the process of moving away from an economy based on drug trafficking to one that is sound and healthy, based on lawful business and investments. But this takes time; in fact, it takes years. Meanwhile, everyone suffers, Christians and unbelievers alike. In our church, as in others, we have people who have not been paid for more than ten months and others who have lost their employment. In the process, the church suffers too, since it doesn't receive its usual tithes and offerings. But at the same time, we learn to help those who suffer.

We prayed against corruption—and greater corruption was exposed. No sooner had we repented before the Lord for all the graft in our country than new scandals rocked our nation. Many senators had been secretly pocketing huge sums of money while the people lacked their sustenance. Scarcely had we recovered from the shock of this news when a similar exposé came out about congressmen.

We prayed for an end to the violence—and guerrilla and paramilitary forces stepped up their attacks. Although the number of murders plummeted after our first *vigilia*, the kidnappings continue, as do the threats of violence, social unrest, and killings. With unemployment so high and no social welfare program, robberies and violence have increased. This situation has resulted in some two million Colombians emigrating to other countries.

To the natural eye, it would seem that the situation has only grown worse. Yet unless corruption is first exposed to the light, we cannot deal with it. It is like a deep, festering wound that a physician must lance in order to drain out all the infection. Before the wound is cleaned, everything must come to the surface. Only then does healing begin. In the same way, what appeared to be devastating news was, in reality, God answering our prayers. If we look beyond the newspaper reports, we see God at work in response to the prayers of His people.

So many times we go through a period of suffering that is actually a result of answered prayer, although we don't recognize it as such. It is God turning upside down a false socio-economic situation that has no solid foundation and had to collapse at some point. When we are in this kind of transition, we have to see beyond the immediate circumstances and gain a higher perspective.

A Matter of Timing

When Moses returned after 40 years in the desert and explained to the elders of Israel that the Lord was going to deliver them from Egypt, they bowed down and worshiped the Lord who had heard their cries and groaning. But the grateful worship changed completely after Moses' first encounter with Pharaoh. Things had not gotten better as expected. In fact, they had gotten much worse, and the people of Israel wished that Moses had never come at all!

May God deliver us from being shortsighted—from demanding immediate gratification like the rebellious children of Israel: "For I know the plans I have for you," declares the LORD, "plans to prosper you and not to harm you, plans to give you a hope and a future" (Jeremiah 29:11). Sometimes God's promises are delayed only to display His great and awesome power and to increase our faith and teach us perseverance, important lessons for the last days.

In the first 14 chapters of Exodus, ten times the Lord speaks of making Himself known through all that happened in Egypt. He sent all those judgments so that Pharaoh, Pharaoh's officials, the Egyptians, the surrounding nations, the Israelites, their children, and their children's children would "know that I am the LORD!" He was revealing His awesome character, His love for Israel, and His hatred for sin.

We must break our old mindsets and renew our minds, our ways of thinking. We need God's perspective in all that we face in life. It is only then that we can be transformed (Romans 12:2).

In Cali, we have assurance that our city is on the road to transformation because God's church is being transformed. And when God's people are transformed, the city will be transformed as well. It is just a matter of time.

See the Invisible

...we fix our eyes not on what is seen, but on what is unseen.
For what is seen is temporary, but what is unseen is eternal.
2 Corinthians 4:18

If we are going to participate effectively in what God is doing today, our natural vision is not sufficient. We need to learn to see with our spiritual eyes, if His will is to be accomplished through us. What we see, or how we see, will determine our actions.

The problem is that God's ways, being higher than ours, do not always make sense to us (Isaiah 55:8–11). He is sovereign over all. He does what He pleases (Psalm 115:3) and His plan cannot be thwarted (Job 42:2). Therefore, we need to learn His ways and think His thoughts in order to flow with what He is doing. We need to see with spiritual eyes. As Paul tells us in Romans 12:2, we must be transformed into the image of His Son, rather than remain conformed to this world.

As an illustration, let me ask a question about the vegetables in Almolonga, Guatemala, as described in The Sentinel Group's *Transformations* video. The carrots in Almolonga are the size of a man's forearm. To most of us that is an enormous carrot. But what size are they to God? Are they large, medium, or small? I think they are normal carrots and that what we usually think of as "normal" falls far short of what a carrot should be. And so it is in many areas of life; we have accepted many things as normal that fall far beneath what the Lord has for us.

What Do You See?

Before giving His prophets a message, the Lord checked their vision. After they described what they saw, he explained its meaning and then gave them a word for Israel.

"What do you see, Jeremiah?" He asked repeatedly (Jeremiah 1:11, 13; 24:3). First, it was the branch of an almond tree. Next it was a boiling pot, tilting away from the north, directed toward Judah. Later it was two baskets of figs, one with good fruit and the other with bad.

"What do you see, Amos?" He asked (Amos 7:8, 8:2). Amos saw a basket of ripe fruit, later a plumb line.

"What do you see, Zechariah?" He asked (Zechariah 4:2, 5:2, 5). Zechariah saw a solid gold lamp stand with a bowl and seven lights fed by oil from two olive trees. Next he saw a flying scroll, and then a measuring basket.

What we see with our spiritual eyes is extremely important, for with the correct vision we will also have a message from God. And that message will determine how we act.

Seeing with Spiritual Eyes

The Bible is full of accounts that emphasize the importance of seeing with our spiritual eyes. David could kill Goliath because he saw him as puny in relation to the mighty God of Israel—whereas his countrymen saw themselves as puny compared to Goliath's towering size and strength (1 Samuel 17).

When Samuel anointed David king of Israel, he learned that God does not look on the outward appearance but on the heart (1 Samuel 16:7).

Joseph forgave his brothers because he knew, or saw, that what they had intended for harm God had intended for good, for the saving of many lives (Genesis 50:20).

Jesus saw well beyond what His natural eyes could capture. Isaiah 11:3b says of Him, "He will not judge by what He sees with His eyes, or decide by what He hears with His ears." He had a vision of joy that enabled Him to endure the shame and bear the cross. What was it that He saw in the midst of that dark hour? He saw His Father's pleasure in His obedience, and that was enough to make Him endure the cross. He delighted to do His will; His very food was to do the will of His Father, and His obedience meant our salvation.

This is what we must learn as His church. We need to understand God's ways, then we will know how to flow with His plan. We need to see and perceive His working.

In 2 Kings 6:15–20, we read how Elijah warned Israel about Syria's plans against them. The Syrian army, with its massive array of horses and chariots, completely surrounded the city of Dothan, with the intent to capture the prophet. Looking with their natural eyes, the Syrians claimed victory. Elijah's servant, looking with natural eyes, was filled with fear. Then the prophet prayed that God would open his servant's eyes so that he could see what was really happening. Only when his servant looked with his spiritual eyes could he see the hills full of the Lord's armies.

Then God blinded the natural eyes of the Syrians and opened them only after they were captured by the Israelites. First, spiritually blind, the Syrian army was made physically blind. God brought the enemy's spiritual blindness into the natural realm! And He wants to open our spiritual eyes so that we, seeing clearly, will flow in His will, bringing the spiritual reality into the natural realm.

Spiritual Blindness Paralyzes

When God brought the children of Israel out of Egypt with mighty signs and wonders, He led them to a place where they were hemmed in by mountains on both sides, the Red Sea before them, and the Egyptian army closing in on them swiftly from behind. What did they see? They saw only death with their natural eyes. Terrified, they cried out to the Lord (Exodus 14). They completely forgot the wonderful demonstrations of God's mighty power that had brought them safe thus far.

If they had seen with their spiritual eyes, they would have realized that the Lord was about to destroy the Egyptian army. This crisis was yet another opportunity for God to show His awesome power. This crisis was actually the means of their salvation, not their destruction! If we see only with our natural eyes, we will easily be deceived. The temporal is not the true reality.

Spiritual Blindness Causes Loss of Faith

When Moses sent out the 12 spies to scout the Promised Land (Numbers 13), they all saw the same physical landscape and people —a land flowing with milk and honey, large fortified cities, and powerful giants. Nevertheless, Joshua and Caleb had the spiritual vision to see that these powerful "giants" were nothing compared to the awesome power of their mighty God. Caleb said, "We should go up and take possession of the land, for we can certainly do it" (Numbers 13:30). The other ten, seeing the giants, refused: "We can't attack those people; they are stronger than we are. ...We seemed like grasshoppers in our own eyes, and we looked the same to them" (verses 31, 33). They were looking with their own natural eyes and lost the vision God had given them.

The bad report of these ten men swiftly permeated the entire camp of Israelites. All night long the people wept and complained against Moses and Aaron. "If only we had died in Egypt! Or in this desert! Why is the LORD bringing us to this land only to let us fall by the sword?" (Numbers 14:1–3). They decided to return to Egypt and would actually have stoned Joshua and Caleb had not the Lord intervened.

Perhaps the saddest part of this story is found in Joshua

2:9–11, where we learn that these powerful "giants" had been "melting in fear" because of the Israelites. They had heard how the Lord had dried up the Red Sea so the Israelites could escape from Egypt, how the Israelites had completely destroyed the two kings of the Amorites. As Rahab told the spies, "I know that the LORD has given this land to you and that a great fear of you has fallen on us, so that all who live in this country are melting in fear because of you" (Joshua 2:9). She continued, "our hearts melted and everyone's courage failed because of you, for the LORD your God is God in heaven above and on the earth below" (Joshua 2:11).

What a tragedy! The enemy saw the Almighty God of Israel far more clearly than the people of God did! May we be a people who know our God and see with spiritual eyes, focusing on Him and His sovereignty, rather than on our circumstances.

With all the opposition that Moses endured from his own people, he had to have a vision that went beyond the natural. Moses persevered because he saw the Invisible One, as the writer to the Hebrews tells us.

Stephen, too, saw the Invisible One when he was being stoned. He saw the glory of God, and Jesus standing at the right hand of God (Acts 7:55–56). Because he had spiritual sight, he could die righteously (Acts 8). We need to see Him, both to live and to die.

Spiritual Vision Makes Us Overcomers

In the third year of the drought, Elijah had a valiant confrontation with wicked King Ahab and the prophets of Baal (1 Kings 18:16–46). The Lord displayed His mighty power by sending fire out of the heavens to consume Elijah's evening sacrifice in front of the people of Israel and the frustrated, bleeding prophets of Baal. Just minutes before, the people had faltered between two opinions. Now they were exclaiming, "The LORD, He is God!" But it still had to rain. Before Elijah even went to pray, he told the wicked King Ahab to go home because "there is the sound of a heavy rain" (verse 41). It wasn't yet raining, but the prophet "heard" the sound of the rain.

Then Elijah climbed to the top of Mount Carmel. He bowed down with his head between his knees "birthing" rain in prayer. He prayed expectantly, waiting on the Lord. Six times he sent his servant to look for a rain cloud in the sky, and six times the servant returned, reporting nothing. Finally, on the seventh time, "a cloud as small as a man's hand" appeared. Then Elijah sent his servant to tell Ahab to "go down before the rain stops you."

I wonder if such a small cloud would have satisfied us, as it did Elijah? To Elijah that tiny cloud represented such a heavy rain that he knew it could have prevented Ahab from reaching home. He had spiritual eyes and could see what God was doing. What he saw caused him to take immediate action. Would that small cloud have discouraged us? Or would we have seen a heavy rain?

Just a few people of faith, meeting together in prayer for their community, are powerful. Never despise the day of small things. As the Lord begins answering those prayers, others will be drawn in. Don't wait until you have a large group or representatives from all the churches. Just two or three people united in prayer and fasting are enough to ignite a fire. We have seen this principle work over and over again in united prayer and city transformation.

God Fulfills Promises

Often the Lord gives us a promise and then brings circumstances into our lives that make it seem impossible for these promises to be fulfilled. He is checking our vision in order to strengthen our faith.

God promised Abraham that his descendants would be like the sand of the sea and the stars of the sky, but Abraham's wife Sarah was sterile. Many years later, when both were far past childbearing age, Isaac was born to Sarah. They learned that *there is nothing too hard for God.*

Isaac inherited these promises given to Abraham. However, he too married a woman who was barren. Only after Isaac's intercession did the Lord intervene and open Rebekah's womb so that she bore two sons, Esau and Jacob.

As a youth, Joseph had two dreams in which God promised him that he would one day be raised up above his brothers, who would bow to him. But the next thing he knew, he was a slave in another country, where he spent several years in prison. He was far from his family and seemingly far from the promises of God. But through it all, the Lord was preparing the vessel to fulfill God's promises. He was shaping and preparing Joseph to be a leader.

What We Saw at Julio's Death

People often ask why our family didn't leave Cali after Julio's death. Certainly, we had the opportunity to leave, and the Lord could have used those circumstances to give us new direction. But we had a vision.

In 1979 the Lord gave my husband a vision for Colombia which we treasured in our hearts. He saw a small river, which began to grow and to build up momentum. Suddenly a huge barrier, like a massive wall, appeared directly in its path. By then it was a rushing river that crashed against the wall and fell back. But it then returned with a resounding boom and knocked the wall down and became a mighty forceful river flowing through the city. Then the Lord spoke to him, saying that this was the move of God in Cali. Years later, just months before Julio's death, the Lord spoke to him again about the move of God in our city.

When Julio was martyred, our family saw his death as the prelude to the promised move of God. To us his death announced the beginning of the move of the Spirit for which we had been praying. We knew we had to stay. To leave would have been to quit before seeing what God had for our city. We "saw" something that could not be seen with the natural eye. We did not know exactly what the Lord had in store for us, but we knew it would glorify Him.

We recognized God's sovereignty in allowing Julio's death and knew that He had entrusted us with the incredible privilege of giving our dearest as a martyr. This caused us to feel an awesome responsibility to walk closely with the Lord, so that He could use Julio's death, and us, for His purposes.

If only we allow the Lord, He will take the greatest tragedy and turn it into something for His glory. In the process, He gives us the grace to serve Him victoriously in spite of the pain.

Maintain Spiritual Vision

The more we come to truth, the more we will learn to see with our spiritual eyes. The Psalmist tells us in 19:8b, "The commands of the Lord are radiant, giving light to the eyes." Seeing Him is what keeps us centered and stable during the difficult seasons of life, as it did for Moses. But sin will keep us from having the spiritual sight that we so desperately need. "Woe to us, for we have sinned! Because of this our hearts are faint, because of these things our eyes grow dim..." (Lamentations 5:16b, 17). In Matthew 13:15 we read, "For this people's heart has become calloused; they hardly hear with their ears, and they have closed their eyes." Sin will cause our hearts to become calloused; we will have difficulty hearing and seeing correctly.

Jesus gave sight to the blind; it was one of the most commonly reported miracles that He performed during His ministry on earth. Today He has the salve to cleanse our eyes so we can see clearly (Revelation 3:18). As He healed those who were physically blind, He is still opening the eyes of the blind today. Then, when trials come, we can "fix our eyes not on what is seen, but on what is unseen. For what is seen is temporary, but what is unseen is eternal" (2 Corinthians 4:18). Let us fix our eyes on Jesus (Hebrews 12:2) who alone can make us see as we ought.

How Do You See Your City?

As we ask the Lord to open our eyes, He will begin to reveal His vision for our community and we will begin to see things in a different way. God has a heart for cities, even those lost in great sin. In fact, the Lord loved the wicked city of Nineveh so much, He not only knew the people but cared for their cattle. The people were so lost they couldn't tell their right hand from their left. Yet He sent Jonah to call them to repentance so that they would be saved. He loves our communities!

Each community has redemptive qualities that God wants to use for His kingdom. One of Cali's redemptive qualities has resulted in the *vigilias*. When I came here, I found out that Cali was well known for its parties. I was surprised to find that the people began at around 10 o'clock at night and continued until 7 o'clock in the morning, or later. The people would dance and drink the whole night through, even taking their small children with them. The children would curl up in chairs fast asleep in the midst of all the noise. Before the believers came to know the Lord, that was their lifestyle. Today, having found the Lord, they find great joy in praying and praising the Lord all through the night. For them it is redemptive; instead of being a people who party all night, they are a people who pray all night. God has redeemed this cultural trait for His glory.

Other redemptive qualities were exhibited through the drug cartel, which had developed the most sophisticated means to export cocaine. These creative and organizational gifts are from God, and we believe they will be used one day to export the gospel to other nations.

These are only two examples, but there are many others. Each community has its own characteristics that the Lord will redeem for His glory, just as each church has its own calling to reflect part of the manifold character of God. When our spiritual eyes are opened, we will recognize them, even if these gifts are now used for evil. Once we see the gifts, we will know how to pray. Who would have thought that the Lord would have done such a work in Cali, such a sinful, lost community? But He is using the redemptive qualities of our city to change it.

May He open our eyes to see, so that we may believe and pray intelligently for His will to be done.

Experience Joy and Blessing in Trials

You intended to harm me, but God intended it for good....
Genesis 50:20

It was one of those times when everything seemed to go wrong. Landslides damaged our property. Spiritual opposition against us intensified. Our church received serious death threats. In the midst of all this, one phrase kept playing over and over again in my mind: *"Count it pure joy! Count it pure joy!"* I knew that only His Spirit could teach me to count these trials "pure joy," so I asked the Lord to help me. As a result, the Lord taught me many things.

When we go through trials, we usually pray, "Lord, I know You can get me through this! We will make it through together somehow!" We squeeze through the trial, barely surviving, then sigh with relief when it's over. But that is not pure joy. You may say, "Let's not get fanatical about this! How *can* you 'count it pure joy'? It hurts. Things are going wrong. I don't feel any joy!"

In the book of James, we learn the reason why we can count it all joy when we go through trials: "because you know that the testing of your faith develops perseverance. Perseverance must finish its work so that you may be mature and complete, not lacking anything" (James 1:3–4).

The Lord does not want us to lack anything. He wants to bring us to maturity. In order to do this, He must develop perseverance in us. Perseverance is not developed overnight; it comes through patience. And patience is learned through trials. Trials, then, are the means God uses to develop His character in us and to help us grow into spiritual maturity. Then we will know Him better and be able to reflect Him better to a lost world. The Lord takes our bitter experiences and turns them into something sweet, something refreshing.

Where Can I Flee?

When going through trials, we tend to look for an escape from the discomfort and pain. David also wanted to flee from his troubles:

I said, "Oh, that I had the wings of a dove!
…I would flee far away and stay in the desert;
I would hurry to my place of shelter,
far from the tempest and storm."
     Psalm 55: 6–8

David's initial thought was to flee, but he decided not to run away. He decided instead to run to the Lord. He went on to say in that same psalm: "But I call to God, and the LORD saves me" (verse 16).

David repeats the same thought in Psalm 11:1, and again he chooses to make the Lord his refuge. He knew the Lord was his only refuge, so how could he run away?

In the LORD I take refuge.
How then can you say to me:
"Flee like a bird to your mountain."
     Psalm 11:1

How many times we run to our "mountains," trying to find refuge in them. We run to a friend for assurance. We move to a different location for safety. We rely on our bank account for security. We hide in that place of refuge. But nothing—and no one—can be a refuge for us like Jesus! Everything else is unstable and insecure.

God of the Mountains—and Valleys

David asks, "When the foundations are being destroyed, what is the Righteous One doing?" (verse 3). In the verses that follow David answers his own question:

The LORD is in His holy temple;
The LORD is on His heavenly throne,
He observes the sons of men;
His eyes examine them.
The LORD examines the righteous, ...
    Psalm 11:4–5

When everything seems to be falling apart, what is God doing? We all wonder about this when going through difficulties. But even when the foundations are being destroyed, God is sovereign, ruling on His heavenly throne.

Having established the fact of God's sovereignty, David goes on to say that the Lord is testing us. In other words, He is allowing us to go through certain situations in life to see how willing we are to trust and follow Him. Do we love Him and trust Him only when it is convenient and comfortable? Or do we also love Him and trust Him in the midst of tragedy, when there seems to be no way out?

Is our trust and devotion to Him based on who God is? Or is it based on our circumstances?

Our God is the God of the mountains and the God of the valleys. The king of Syria, Ben-Hadad, found that out when the Syrians attacked the Israelites (1 Kings 20). When Israel won the first battle in the hills, the Syrians decided it was because the God of Israel was a "god of the hills" (verse 23). So they attacked again;

this time they were in the plains. The Syrian army covered the countryside, and the Israelites were like two flocks of goats. The Syrians were sure of their victory. But again Israel prevailed. God wanted to show the Syrians—and Israel—that He is the God of the mountains as well as the valleys.

Yes, the Lord is the God of our wonderful mountain-top experiences, but He is also the God of our difficult valleys. In Job 38:1 we learn that it was out of the storm that the Lord spoke to Job.

Refiner's Fire

At the same time that the Lord is testing us through trials, He is also refining and purifying us. He wants to test the genuineness of our faith. Peter writes that the purpose is that our faith "may be proved genuine and may result in praise, glory, and honor when Jesus Christ is revealed" (1 Peter 1:6–7).

When Daniel's three friends were bound and thrown into the fiery furnace by Nebuchadnezzar (Daniel 3:19), the Lord walked in the fire with them. When they were released from the furnace, the flames had only served to burn the ropes that had bound them! Not a hair of their heads was singed. The flames had neither touched them nor their clothes, nor did the smell of smoke cling to them.

If we allow the Lord to walk with us in our trials, these trials will refine us and free us, as that fire did for those three young men, and there will be no telltale scent of smoke.

What Are You Holding Onto?

My husband was greatly used by God in many South American nations. In fact, the course of history was changed in his native Bolivia when the president opened the doors for Julio to preach the gospel. Previously, Bolivia had been one of the most difficult nations to reach.

God used miracles to fill the stadiums, which couldn't contain the crowds of up to 85,000 people. The Lord also used Julio's ministry to open doors to the gospel in other countries. In Medellin, Colombia, the newspapers reported 100,000 people in attendance at one of the meetings.

God not only used Julio in a magnificent way but also promised even greater things ahead. In one promise, the Lord assured us that these crowds would be nothing compared to the numbers of people Julio would touch in the future. Before this promise was fulfilled, Julio died. But that didn't stop the Lord. After Julio's death, tens of thousands have been ministered to through his testimony in the Promise Keepers' video. Millions more have been touched by his life through the *Transformations* video. The Lord's promise was fulfilled, but certainly not in the way we had expected. The Lord always fulfills His promises but many times it is not *when* we expect or in the *way* we expect. God does it according to *His* plan and *His* perfect timing.

We all have promises from God that we treasure in our hearts. We are waiting expectantly for that day when the dream or promise will become a reality. Yet when the Lord's promises to us are not fulfilled in our time frame, it seems as though He has forgotten. He hasn't forgotten; He is calling us to die to them. The Lord is testing our hearts, our motives, and our faith. Promises cannot mean more than obedience to His will, and they cannot be the motivating factor that drives us. Our source must be God.

Many times the Lord asks us to lay down the very answer to our prayers and dreams, risking the chance of losing them forever, just as He asked Abraham to sacrifice Isaac on the altar. But when we do sacrifice that dream or promise, He brings something even greater out of its death because of our obedience. That is when we have to believe in the sovereignty of God, whether it makes sense to us or not.

Jesus was the promised Messiah, the one for whom the Jews

had been waiting for centuries! He was the answer they had been praying for and, according to the disciples' perspective, He wasn't supposed to die! His kingdom was eternal. Yet, in accordance with His Father's will, He chose to die and the disciples' hopes died as well on that day—temporarily. They were saddened and confused, unaware of the greatest victory ever attained. Jesus took a loss that we might gain. Because of His death and resurrection, we have life. He gave us authority, a commission, an abundant life. Yet it was disguised in a tragedy, in a loss.

Jonah writes: "Those who cling to worthless idols forfeit the grace that could be theirs" (Jonah 2:8). If we hold on to anyone or anything other than the Lord, it is an idol and it prevents us from receiving from God the grace He wants to give us. Only when we lay down every promise, every dream, every desire at His feet, only then will we receive the grace we need to do His will and bring Him pleasure.

Lord, I Want to Know You More

How often we sing and pray, "Lord, I want to know You more! Lord, I want to see Your face!" If the Lord should answer, "All right, I am going to reveal Myself to you as the God of all comfort," we respond: "No, no, no! I want to know a *different* aspect of You!"

We like to choose what God is going to reveal to us. But He allows us to go through sorrow so that He can reveal Himself to us as the "God of all comfort." After we have walked through sorrow, we can minister to the hurting in a deeper way because we are ministering from the revelation of the God of all comfort. Any Christian can talk about comfort with academic knowledge, but it is when we walk through situations that call for His comfort that the revelation comes, and that revelation is far greater than the pain we are experiencing. How can He be "the God of all comfort" to us if we do not go through sorrow and need to be comforted? If God wants to reveal Himself to us as our Provider, then He will allow us to go through a period of material need so that we can know Him as our Provider. The Lord allows trials in our lives so that we can know Him more intimately. The awesome revelation of His person enables us to let go of everything but Him. The Lord promises that "upright men will see His face" (Psalm 11:7). God uses every opportunity to reveal Himself to us. If we trust Him in the midst of all our trials, we will see His face. His revelation is more important than our present condition. A revelation of God will let us know Him better. It will mature us and allow us to reflect Him to others. There is so much we don't know about Him that He wants to share with us.

In Psalm 84:5 David says, "Blessed are those whose strength is in You, who have their hearts set on pilgrimage." David knew that strength comes when we get God's perspective. He knew, just like Abraham did, that he was just passing through. Abraham wasn't even looking for Canaan, the land that the Lord had promised him. He was looking for something eternal (Hebrews 11:10).

When our eyes are placed on Jesus, everything else falls into the right place, and we see things through His perspective. When we understand that we are just pilgrims in this world, that we are only passing through, our priorities change. The things that weigh so heavily on us aren't as important as before. They don't affect us in the same way. We begin to see and handle things differently and knowing Him in everything becomes the priority.

Joseph's Example

Joseph's life stands out as an encouragement to all who are struggling through valleys of despair and tragedy. He is a model of how God uses valley experiences to shape our character and prepare us for His call on our lives. Genesis chapters 37–50 show us how Joseph bore fruit out of pain and sorrow.

Joseph was Jacob's favorite son. He was the eleventh of Jacob's sons, the first son of Rachel. Jacob gave him a robe of many colors which in ancient times represented the father's intention of bestowing on his son a double blessing. When Joseph was a teenager, he had two dreams revealing his rise to a position of powerful leadership and his future elevation over his brothers and family. All these things, which Joseph told his brothers, only intensified their jealousy and hatred of him. Although they originally planned to kill him, they were finally persuaded to sell him to Ishmaelite traders en route to Egypt.

There in Egypt, a land with a different culture, language, and religion, Joseph was sold into slavery. It seemed even more impossible than ever before that he would see the promises of God realized. Humanly speaking, there was almost no chance at all.

Nevertheless, God prospered him, granting him favor in the eyes of Potiphar, one of Pharaoh's officers and the captain of the palace guard. Potiphar made Joseph his personal servant and put him in charge of his household. But then, because Joseph was righteous and faithful to God, he was unjustly thrown into prison, based on a false accusation by Potiphar's wife. There "they bruised his feet with shackles, his neck was put in irons" (Psalm 105:18). Yet God blessed Joseph. Eventually he was put in charge of the prisoners. His hopes rose when both the king's cupbearer and his chief baker had dreams and came to Joseph for an interpretation. But these hopes were dashed again when the cupbearer forgot his promise to speak to the Pharaoh in Joseph's behalf. Yet all during Joseph's years in prison, God was preparing him.

At God's appointed time, the Lord gave Pharaoh two dreams that neither the wise men nor magicians could interpret. At long last, the cupbearer remembered Joseph, and Joseph had the opportunity to interpret these dreams for the king. He warned him of the seven years of plenty, to be followed by seven years of famine, and recommended a plan to prepare for the years of famine. Impressed with Joseph's wisdom and discernment, Pharaoh appointed Joseph second in command to himself and in charge over all of Egypt (Genesis 41:39–43).

Joseph had to endure these trials for 13 years before God elevated him to a position of leadership. During that period, he learned many lessons. Joseph had proven himself faithful in the face of adversity, injustice and betrayal. He had trusted the Lord and hadn't become bitter or angry because of his trials. Through it all, God was preparing him for his own purposes.

Forgetting the Pain of the Past

When Pharaoh made Joseph second in his kingdom, he blessed him with a wife, and Joseph had two sons by her. Manasseh was the first born, whose name means "forgetting"— "because God has made me forget all my trouble and all my father's household" (Genesis 41:51). He was able to forget his sorrow and pain and get a new start in life.

It is wonderful when we can leave the past behind and move on with God's plan and purpose for our life. There are Christians today who have lived through unbelievably difficult situations, possibly as victims of persecution, or child abuse, or as a result of having made the wrong choices, but absolutely everything is new when Jesus steps in. He is the only one who can make us forget the pain and sorrow. This is not denial—it is truly leaving the pain behind and experiencing the cleansing and healing that the Father has provided for us through our Lord's sacrifice.

Fruitful in the Land of Suffering

The name of Joseph's second son, Ephraim, means "fruitful in the land of my suffering" (Genesis 41:52). Joseph had learned that there is more than forgetting the pain of the past. We can take our suffering and allow it to produce fruit. God was making Joseph fruitful in the land of his suffering.

Years later, when Jacob was very old, Joseph took his sons to his father, that Jacob might bless them. Jacob himself had been the second-born son and knew that the "double portion" of blessing usually belonged to the firstborn. Nevertheless, he laid his right hand on Ephraim's head, the younger son. Joseph tried to correct his father, but Jacob knew what he was doing. He knew the older son would serve the younger. Manasseh would be blessed, but the "double portion" would fall on Ephraim; he would be greater than Manasseh.

It is wonderful to walk in the Manasseh blessing of "forgetting" our pain. But there is more than forgetting. The Lord can teach us to bear fruit out of our pain and sorrow. That is where the double blessing is, and its fruit will bless many. That's where the anointing lies.

When Jacob's sons all gathered around him before he died, he spoke a blessing over each one (Genesis 49). Over Joseph, he spoke these words: "Joseph is a fruitful bough...his branches run over the wall" (Genesis 49:22, NKJV). Because Joseph allowed the Lord to use his suffering and pain to produce fruit, his bough went "over the wall," blessing not only his own family but a great many others as well.

In difficult times of suffering and pain, the Lord wants to reveal Himself to us in a new way. He is maturing us so that we may better reflect Him to others and become a blessing to them. He will produce fruit from the land of our suffering, if we only allow Him. He gives us the grace, enabling us to be all that we should be and to do all that He calls us to do, when we allow Him.

Isaiah tells us that if we trust Him, He will keep us in perfect peace and our mind will be steadfast because we trust in Him (Isaiah 26:3). The result of trusting Him is a steadfast mind. When we go through problems, we have an anchor in Jesus. He gives us a different perspective. When we rise up to higher levels with Him, our perspective changes. We can then look down from a higher place, and the problem looks a lot smaller as a result.

The Psalmist writes, "He who sacrifices thank offerings honors Me, and he prepares the way so that I may show him the salvation of God" (Psalm 50:23). When we come before the Lord and offer Him thank offerings, even though we are going through difficult times, we are preparing the way for the Lord to show us His salvation.

In Psalm 84, we learn that our tears can be collected to become a well that refreshes others:

Blessed are those whose strength is in You,
who have set their hearts on pilgrimage.
As they pass through the Valley of Baca (weeping),
they make it a place of springs ...
They go from strength to strength.
    Psalm 84:5–7

Hosea 2:15 tells how the Lord "will make the Valley of Achor [trouble] a door of hope." The Lord is able to open a door of hope in the midst of our pain and tragedy! The enemy wants us to become bitter, resentful, and focused on our problem, our defeat, and our loss. But if we look to the Lord our tears can be a source of refreshing for others and in our trouble we can find a door of hope. The land of our suffering can become fruitful, and a blessing.

When trials come, the Lord is about to reveal Himself in a new way. We can say, "Lord, here I am. It doesn't make any sense to me, but here I am. I want a revelation of You! I want to know You more! I want to learn!" Joseph forgave his brothers. He saw how God's hand had been on him all during those years. "You intended to harm me, but God intended it for good to accomplish what is now being done, the saving of many lives" (Genesis 50:20). Anything that happens to us, He has allowed because He knows He can bring good from it.

We can count it all joy then, not because the suffering and pain go away, but because we know that He is doing something in our lives that will bring glory to His name. That joy alone outweighs anything else. Our faith rests securely in Jesus.

Activate Faith through Obedience

"It really doesn't matter who you are.
All that really matters is who I am.
Just be obedient to all I ask of you."

M ost Christians desire to see their city transformed by the Lord. Yet the instrument that He uses, the church, is often disunited and seems to lack the faith needed for such a move. There are individual leaders and ministries that seem to move out in faith and power, but not a united city-church. I remember as a teenager longing to see the church function as it did in the book of Acts. If the church needed to manifest the powerful presence of Jesus in its earliest days, wouldn't it need even more for the last days? What do we need to do in order to have the power of God that will move a city, nation, continent, and the world?

We often pray for the presence of the Lord to come down, but that cannot happen in any significant way unless we become a people of obedience. Obedience is one of the ingredients that attracts the presence and glory of God.

In Exodus 39 and 40 the Bible says that when the Israelites built the tabernacle they "had done all the work just as the LORD had commanded Moses. Moses inspected the work and saw that they had done it just as the LORD had commanded.... And so Moses finished the work. *Then* the cloud covered the Tent of Meeting, and the glory of the LORD filled the tabernacle. Moses could not enter the Tent of Meeting because the cloud had settled upon it. And the glory of the LORD filled the tabernacle."

The purpose of carefully building the tabernacle according to the Lord's specifications was that the glory and presence of the Lord could fill it (Leviticus 9:5, 6). Leviticus 9 and 10 tell us that the glory of the Lord appeared to all the people. Fire actually came out from His presence and consumed the sacrifice that they were offering.

Choose Life or Death

As the priests worshiped before the Lord, Nadab and Abihu, Aaron's sons, offered "unauthorized" fire before the Lord. They disobeyed the Law and died. Obedience always brings life and disobedience always brings death. That is why Moses told the people that they had to choose between life and death by choosing obedience or disobedience, respectively: "...I have set before you life and death, blessings and curses. Now choose life, so that you and your children may live and that you may love the LORD your God, listen to His voice, and hold fast to Him. For the LORD is your life...." (Deuteronomy 30:19, 20). If we want the presence of God in our lives and communities, we must walk in obedience to Him. This begins as each of us chooses obedience and life.

Obedience Gives Us Authority

Obedience is walking in submission to God's will and ways. When we walk in obedience, we will also walk in authority. Jesus Himself learned obedience by the things He suffered, and later, at His glorious ascension, He tells us that all authority has been given to Him (Hebrews 5:8 and Matthew 28:18). There is no authority without submission.

When we live in submission and obedience, we receive the covering of the One over us, and the authority of that Person flows through us to others. In Luke 7:1–10 we read of the centurion who understood this principle, saying, "For I myself am a man under authority, with soldiers under me. ..." Jesus commended him as a man of great faith.

We all obey someone or something, whether God or a civil authority, parental authority, or simply our own depraved nature. Obedience joins us to the one to whom we are submitted and allows that authority to become ours. We become the servant of whomever we obey (Romans 6:16). In order to be joined to Jesus and have His authority, we must be His obedient servants.

We Must Learn His Ways

We are told that the Israelites could have crossed the desert from Egypt to the Promised Land in only 11 to 14 days. However, the Lord never intended for them to go into the Promised Land immediately after leaving Egypt. God brought them out of Egypt, but then had them stay in the desert for more than a year, perhaps even two, to teach them how they were to live.

After living for over 400 years in Egypt, the Israelites had incorporated much of the Egyptian culture into their own way of life. And they left Egypt as a "mixed multitude." God needed to teach Israel His ways and then bring them into the Promised Land so that they could establish a whole new nation and way of life that He could bless and that would draw other nations to Himself. Had they gone directly from Egypt into the Promised Land, they would have established "New Egypt." He had taken Israel out of Egypt, but He still had to take Egypt out of Israel and teach them His ways.

During this time in the desert, God gave Moses His Law. The Law covered far more than the Ten Commandments with which we are most familiar. It contained a whole way of life for His people. Through obedience, Israel would be blessed, but disobedience would bring a curse. Deuteronomy 28 contains a long list of blessings and curses that would come upon Israel, depending on her choices. All the people had to do was to obey God. It sounds quite simple, but Israel found it too hard.

Who Am I?

In August of 1996 I was attending a leadership retreat in Colorado. The speaker that morning was talking about the importance of having a mission statement. In the preceding 11 months my husband and two of my closest friends had died. Until that time, I hadn't realized how much of my identity depended on those who were closest to me. All of a sudden, I realized that I didn't really know who I was. From my innermost being, I cried out to the group for prayer. I really didn't know who I was without my husband and friends.

I complicated my situation even further by continually reminding myself that I didn't care for women as senior pastors. I even got into discussions with myself about roles. Who was I?

Finally, the Lord settled it for me. He said, "It really doesn't matter who you are. All that really matters is who I am. Just be obedient to all that I ask of you." What a relief it brought to my soul! When I put my eyes on Jesus, I knew there was only one thing I had to consider—knowing and doing His will. It quieted my internal debates. All I had to do was hear from Him and obey. In obedience to Him, I am now a senior pastor and love it. It really doesn't matter if I like women in this role. I am obeying Him, and that is all He is asking me to do.

Obedience Gives Victory

Obedience is the rock that gives us strength to persevere; it gives permanence. We are all familiar with the houses in Matthew 7;

one was built on rock, the other on sand. Both houses could have been built with the same expertise and quality of materials. Both went through the same trials: rains, floods, and winds that blew and beat against them. But they had very different results. The one built on the rock stood firm; the one built on the sand fell in great ruin.

We may think of Jesus as the Rock and that we must build our house on that Rock. This is true. However, in this teaching I believe Jesus is making a different point. Both the wise man and the foolish man heard the words of the Lord. The wise man "did" the word; he obeyed. The foolish man heard, but did not "do" the word. He did not live in obedience to the word he heard. He did not allow his life to be transformed by living in obedience to the word. We need to build our houses on obedience to the Lord. When we do, we will find that we have strength when the storms of life come.

Moses commanded the people to obey so that they would have the strength to go into the Promised Land to possess it. Israel's obedience would allow her to defeat nations that were larger and stronger than she was (Deuteronomy 11:8, 23). The Apostle Paul, in 2 Corinthians 10:5b–6, points out the importance of bringing every thought into captivity to the obedience of Christ and being ready to punish all disobedience when our obedience is fulfilled. When the believer is walking in obedience, he has authority to punish disobedience. Jesus came to destroy the work of the enemy, and we too must walk in victory over the enemy. Obedience to Jesus gives us authority and strength because we are walking under the authority of God, who is the victor. His victory becomes ours.

Obedience Is a Demonstration of Our Faith

Faith isn't as subjective as we often think. It is demonstrated by our obedience. If we obey the Lord, we show our faith in God and dependence on Him. In the same way, when we do our own will, we show faith in our own abilities. Hebrews 3:18 tells us that the Israelites could not enter the Promised Land because of their unbelief. Using the same word in Greek, Hebrews 4:2 tells us that they didn't mix the Word with faith and verses 6 and 11 say this was because of disobedience. Jesus casts this thought in a positive sense, saying that the work of God is to believe, which is to obey (John 6:29). Unbelief and disobedience are one in the same; so are faith and obedience.

Israel was meant to possess the Promised Land but realized that they couldn't do it in their own strength. God wanted to show His strength on behalf of Israel, but because they didn't believe and disobeyed, they could not receive His promise.

When my life was threatened, many Christians commented, "We need to keep you alive." I appreciated their concern, and I certainly would not do anything foolish to put my life or my daughters' lives in jeopardy. But if we are truly convinced that obedience to God is more important than life or death, our emphasis needs to be on helping one another stay in the center of God's will. Dying is not the worst thing that can happen to us. "For to me, to live is Christ and to die is gain" (Philippians 1:21). The very worst thing is to be out of God's will.

In times of danger the Lord may give direction to leave, as He did when Paul went over the Damascus wall in a basket. But He also directed Paul to go to Jerusalem even though there was persecution ahead. Paul's obedience demonstrated his faith in the Lord's direction. Obedience will allow the Lord to give us the grace, strength and authority that we need for every situation.

Abraham, the father of faith, demonstrated his fear of God by obeying Him. That obedience brought blessing to him, his family, and the world. "... all the nations on earth will be *blessed, because you have obeyed me*" (Genesis 22:18). For Abraham, the One who gave him the promise was more important than the promise itself.

The Lord used my husband Julio to reach hundreds of thousands of people in Bolivia with the gospel through signs, miracles, and wonders that accompanied the preaching of the Word. This ministry would have impressed almost any Christian. But one day the Lord said, "I have not called you to fill stadiums, but to do My will." It was a message that was written on his heart.

As a result, Julio ministered as fervently to 25 people as he did to 80,000, and he ministered as fully to a native from the Altiplano (a plateau 14,000 feet above sea level) as he did to the president of the country. He knew that what impressed man wasn't important; his happiness was found in doing the will of the Lord, whether for the masses or individuals.

Obedience Brings Blessing

The Lord longs for our obedience so that He can bless us. "Oh, that their hearts would be inclined to fear Me and keep all My commandments always, so that it might be well with them and with their children forever!" (Deuteronomy 5:29). Obedience demonstrates our faith in God as well as our fear of God, and it brings blessing not only to our lives but to others as well. As we obey Him, we will find that we have faith.

Obedience Activates Faith

In the sixth chapter of Genesis, the Lord told Noah that He was going to destroy the world in a flood. Then He commanded him to build an ark and gave him the directions to build it. The moment Noah started to work on the ark, his knowledge turned into faith through his obedient action.

In Hebrews 11 each person mentioned in faith's "hall of fame" demonstrated their faith through obedience. Rahab, for example, demonstrated her faith by taking in the spies. Obedience breathes life into faith; it activates faith. Otherwise faith is dead (James 2:24).

Obedience Demonstrates Love

It wouldn't mean much to us if our child kept telling us how much he loved us but never obeyed us. 1 Kings 3:3 tells us that

"Solomon showed his love for the LORD by walking according to the statues of his father David...." Jesus says, "If you love Me, you will obey what I command. He who does not love Me will not obey My teaching..." (John 14:15, 24). Love without obedience is an empty emotion; obedience is love in action.

Disobedience Brings Death

Just as obedience brings life and authority, disobedience brings death. King Saul had been commanded by the Lord through Samuel to execute judgment on the Amalekites by warring against them and killing everyone. But Saul didn't fully obey. He saved the king and some of the best animals (1 Samuel 15). Later we read that it was an Amalekite that killed Saul and took his crown (2 Samuel 1).

Because the Israelites believed the evil report from the ten spies, the Lord told them that they would wander in the desert for 40 years. This upset them and in remorse, instead of repentance, they decided to go back to possess Canaan. Although Moses told them not to go because the Lord would not be with them, they insisted and they lost the battle (Numbers 14). We always lose when we act in disobedience and unbelief.

Do Not Be Deceived

Jesus tells us that an outstanding characteristic of the last days will be deception (Matthew 24). Even we Christians allow deception into our lives. The problem is especially troublesome when it involves Christian leaders and pastors. Because we are in the ministry, we spend much time in the Word preparing sermons and Bible studies, or giving counsel. However, many times we don't spend the necessary time in the Word and prayer just seeking Him for who He is.

We can be so familiar with the Word that we assume we are

living it even when we haven't taken the trouble to apply it to our own lives. James tells us that we are to live out the Word, not just hear it. Not heeding this instruction will only lead to self-deception. I frequently ask the Lord in prayer to show me where I am deceived, or where have I become comfortable with a truth without actually living it? The Lord is always faithful to open my eyes to areas of need so that I can adjust my thinking and live according to His Word.

True Christianity is living in obedience to the Lord in every area of our lives. If we want faith for all that is needed in this day and faith to see God move in our communities, we must learn obedience. Living in obedience will activate our faith and give us the authority to accomplish all that the Lord has for us to do. Not only will we be transformed as individuals, we will also be used by the Lord in our communities.

Walk in Humility, the Key to God's Presence

This is the one I esteem: he who is humble
and contrite in spirit, and trembles at my word.
Isaiah 66:2b

Nothing can satisfy us like the presence of the Lord. The psalmist wrote, "As the deer pants for streams of water, so my soul pants for You, O God" (Psalm 42:1). Our spirit calls out for the Lord, and we deeply desire deeper communion with Him. There is nothing like His presence.

Joshua, as a young man serving Moses, knew the value of communion with God. He "did not depart from the tabernacle" (Exodus 33:11, NKJV), because he wanted to remain in the awesome presence of God.

Moses himself refused to go to the Promised Land unless the presence of the Lord went with Israel. God's presence with His people distinguished Israel from all the other nations:

Then Moses said to him, "If your Presence does not go with us,
do not send us up from here. How will anyone know that you
are pleased with me and with your people unless you go with
us? What else will distinguish me and your people from all the
other people on the face of the earth?" Exodus 33:15–16

David, too, loved the presence of God. In fact, the first thing he desired upon becoming king of Israel was to bring back the presence of God. He knew that God's presence would transform everything. And certainly after Saul's reign, Israel needed the presence of the Lord desperately. The ark, the symbol of God's presence, had been taken by the Philistines and later returned to Israel, where it remained in Kiriath Jearim. But if David was going to be king, he wanted the presence of God in Jerusalem.

Thus David began his first project as king: bringing the Ark of the Covenant back to Jerusalem. For this purpose, he followed the procedure that the Philistines had so successfully used. He had the ark loaded on a new cart that was guided by the sons of Abinadab.

As the ark drew near, their joy was unspeakable. They celebrated with all their might before the Lord with the most wonderful worship! It was a great day—until the oxen stumbled. Uzzah reached out to steady it, God struck him down and he died right beside the ark of God! (2 Samuel 6:2–11).

David was troubled and asked, "How can the presence of the Lord ever come to me?" He had to have the presence of the Lord with him in order to be the king. He knew he was to be a worshiper, one who consulted the Lord for his decisions, and one who acted as the mouthpiece of the Lord. Three months later, David brought the ark back, but this time according to the requirements of the Law.

David should have known from the beginning what the Law said about transporting the ark of God. Every new king was to write the Law on a scroll for himself. He was to carry it with him, read it every day, and follow each of its words (Deuteronomy 17:18–18:1). Had David done that, he would have known how to bring the ark to Jerusalem.

Right and godly motives are not enough to bring the presence of God to our lives and communities. We must do things the Lord's way. If we follow the successful programs and designs of the world, we will never have the presence of God in our midst.

Today, our question is the same as David's. How can the presence of God ever come to our city? And the answer is also the same—by following the directions of the Lord. We need to align our lives in true submission to biblical principles, the logos of God. The written Word gives us parameters for Christian living and spiritual growth.

But the Lord also wants to give us specific direction for our individual lives, churches, and communities—the rhema of God. The Lord speaks to us and gives us direction as we read the Word and seek His face.

We have already seen the importance of obedience. But if we are to obey the Lord, we must hear from Him to know what His will is. The Lord never meant for us to be an independent people. The Christian life cannot be lived without God at the center, yet many times we try to live on our own.

Humility is the key to the kind of obedience that will attract the presence of God. I define humility as "total dependence on the Lord," a complete understanding that without Him we can do nothing. The Lord has the key to our cities and communities. It is He who has the answer, and it is He who will show us the way. We know this because the Lord wants to come down to dwell among His people.

Israel's First Lesson in the Desert

One of the first things the Lord taught the people of Israel when they came out of Egypt was humility—dependence on Him. Only a short time after leaving Egypt they complained that the Lord had brought them into the desert to kill them. So the Lord sent bread from heaven. It was called manna, which means, "what is it?" In Exodus 16 we are told that manna resembled white thin flakes, like frost, and tasted like wafers with honey. In the Psalms manna is called "grain from heaven" and "angel's food."

In Deuteronomy 8:1–3 we are told that the Lord sent the manna specifically to teach the Israelites humility, for dependence on Him, for "man does not live by bread alone, but by every word that proceeds out of the mouth of the Lord." Jesus quotes this

verse from Deuteronomy in Matthew 4:4, using rhema for "word."
The Old Testament was written as a shadow of things to come and
to provide examples for us, so it is important that we understand
what the Lord was teaching His people. We need to learn the same
lessons.

After 400 years in Egypt, Israel had a mixed lifestyle. They
worshiped Jehovah but also the gods of Egypt. They needed to
learn a whole new lifestyle of dependence on God—to hear and
obey the Lord alone. They were to be a people set aside for the
Lord. And today we have that same calling—a call to holiness, set
aside for His purposes.

Manna—the *Rhema* of God

Many lessons for us are found in God's instructions to the
children of Israel about manna. From 1 Corinthians 10:3 we learn
that manna also refers to spiritual food. God wanted to teach them
to depend totally on Him. He wanted them to learn that man does
not live by bread alone but by the *rhema* of God; that is, by what
He said every day. We must also have *rhema* for the specific
situations of our lives, churches, and communities.

Manna was supplied each morning, except on the Sabbath. On
the sixth day, the people were to collect enough for the next day
as well. Just as God supplied the children of Israel with physical
food each day, God's *rhema* to us is fresh every morning. He gives
us specifically what we need for that day. After collecting manna
for six days, the people rested on the seventh. Perhaps one day a
week we, too, should think more about what we can offer back to
God instead of what we are going to get from God. If we did, our
concept of corporate gatherings would radically change.

Manna had to be collected. There was work involved, and it was
a daily responsibility (with the exception of the Sabbath).
Although God provided the manna, the people had to go out and
collect it. We, too, must set aside regular time to seek Him and
align ourselves with His purposes.

They had to eat the manna to gain sustenance. When we eat the manna it becomes an integral part of ourselves and God permeates our very being, enabling us to reflect Him to others.

The sun's heat melted the manna. If they waited until the heat of the day to gather manna, it had already melted. When the storms of life come, or when we go through difficult times of persecution, only the manna that has become a part of our lives will sustain us. Too often, Christians in difficult situations suddenly rush out to get their manna. Now God, in His mercy, may have saved some for us. But when we eat manna regularly, the rhema of God will see us through the heat of the day and pressures of life.

Manna couldn't be stored. Leftover manna became infested with maggots and began to smell. Similarly, we cannot store up God's spiritual food, keeping it in our heads without letting it change our lives. If we do, we deceive ourselves (James 1:23–24). We must allow the presence of Jesus and His Word to become an integral part of our lives. Otherwise, when we speak we will leave a stench of maggot-ridden manna rather than the fragrance of fresh bread.

Jesus, the True Bread from Heaven

Jesus tells us that He is the true bread from heaven, "the bread of life which a man may eat and not die, but will live forever" (John 6:25–59). "...Unless you eat the flesh of the Son of Man and drink His blood, you have no life in you. Whoever eats My flesh and drinks My blood has eternal life..." (verses 54–55). Jesus draws a parallel between our relationship with Him and His relationship with His Father: "...I live because of the Father, so the one who feeds on Me will live because of Me" (verse 58).

Many people were offended by these difficult statements and ceased to follow the Lord. The words are difficult for many of us as well. Many Christians want to control their own lives, but we find our real life in the Lord. We must learn, as did the Israelites, that we cannot live by natural bread alone, but only by feeding on him, the fresh word of God for us—the rhema. The Christian life is intended to be a supernatural life in which we partake of Jesus' life.

Throughout the Gospels we read how Jesus spent time in prayer, sometimes early in the morning before dawn, sometimes all night long:

> *The Sovereign Lord has given Me an instructed tongue, to know the word that sustains the weary. He wakens Me morning by morning, wakens My heart to listen like one being taught.*
> Isaiah 50:4

Because of the time Jesus spent in prayer He knew what to do and what to say, for He had received it from His Father in prayer. Jesus Himself says, "...I do nothing on My own; but I speak just what My Father has taught Me. ...I speak these things...I always do what pleases Him" (John 8:28,29). He repeats this idea in John 12:49, 50: "For I did not speak of My own accord, but the Father who sent Me commanded Me what to say and how to say it. I know that His command leads to eternal life. So whatever I say is just what the Father has told Me to say."

Abide in the Vine

In John 15 we are told to abide in Him, because we cannot bear fruit without Him. Any fruit that is to have eternal value must have its source in God. "He who says he abides in Him ought himself also to walk just as He walked" (1 John 2:6, NKJV). Yes, we need to live as He did—in complete dependence on the Father. He is to be our life. That is humility.

The people of Israel were totally dependent on the Lord in the wilderness. They could only move when the cloud or pillar of fire moved. Had they left that covering, they would have died in the desert. They would have died of hunger, had the Lord not provided them with food. God also miraculously provided them with water, and their clothes did not wear out. He was their God and He cared for them. What more could they ask for? There was no other god like *their* God!

God wants us to be His people, as well, and He wants us to allow Him to be the source of our life. We are to feed on Him, to be fully dependent on Him, to do His will in order to have intimate communion with Him and to accomplish His purposes on earth.

Today the whole world applauds independence, and this spirit has infiltrated the church as well. Paul tells us in 2 Timothy 3 that the last days will be characterized by a self-centered, independent, and disobedient yet religious people. These people will have a form of godliness but reject the power to live a godly life. The Lord came to save us from this "perverse generation." Just as the Lord had to take Egypt out of Israel, He has to do the same for the church today. Until we discover that the manna of God is all we really need, we will always have a yearning for the "leeks and garlic" of Egypt.

Humility, or total dependence on the Lord, is absolutely necessary for Him to be able to carry out His plan through us. Too often, Christians have their plans already made and simply ask the Lord to bless them. In His mercy, many times He does just that. However, the Lord is looking for a people that know their God and do His will at any cost. Then His grace will be there to enable us to do whatever He asks us to do. "The Lord gives grace to the humble but opposes the proud" (James 4:6). He gives grace to those whose dependence is on Him but opposes those whose confidence is in themselves.

Sleep Near the Ark

Our hearts needs to be like that of little Samuel. He positioned himself next to the ark so that he could hear from the Lord. As a result, he learned to hear the voice of the Lord at a young age.

In contrast, Eli slept "in his usual place." We also find that his eyes were becoming so weak that he could barely see and he was heavy. Unfortunately, his spiritual eyes were also dim and he was weighed down in the flesh. Because of his condition as the spiritual leader, the Word of the Lord was "rare" in those days and there was no vision. All of Israel was affected (1 Samuel 3:1–3).

Sadly, there are many Eli-type Christians today. If our lives are filled with the things of this world, we will lose vision and become sluggish in the Lord. We need to learn to "sleep by the ark;" that is, to be close to the things of God at all times. We do this by filling our hearts and minds with the Word of God, meditating on the Word, spending time in prayer and fasting, walking in holiness, and having a grateful heart, among others. Paul underscores this point in Colossians 3:15–17:

> Let the peace of Christ rule in your hearts, since as members of one body you were called to peace. And be thankful. Let the word of Christ dwell in you richly as you teach and admonish one another with all wisdom, and as you sing psalms, hymns and spiritual songs with gratitude in your hearts to God. And whatever you do, whether in word or deed, do it all in the name of the Lord Jesus, giving thanks to God the Father through Him.

Foreign Gods in the Temple

In the Old Testament we read that the Israelites took foreign gods into the temple of God. They actually worshiped Jehovah and other gods at the same time. It seems so ludicrous, yet many times we worship the Lord and, at the same time, have idols in our lives. And we seem to be comfortable with these idols.

We make decisions based on finances instead of first seeking the Lord's will, allowing finances to be a source of confirmation. Or we follow what others tell us instead of first praying to God for guidance. Our dependence cannot be on people or circumstances, but must be on the Lord.

Leaders often create programs to bring people to their churches, rather than seeking the Lord for His direction. They assume that a large church is a successful church. There are many programs seen in other churches that are good and appealing. They may be exactly what the Lord designed for that church, but is that what He wants for ours?

I have been in a church that took on a successful discipleship program that they saw in another church. The original church started their program in fasting and prayer after having heard from the Lord. The program strengthened that church because God was the source of it. The second church seemed successful and grew numerically, but became so program-oriented that one could sense the lack of prayer and passion for the Lord. True success can only be measured by whether we have done His will. The Lord's evaluation system is different from the world's.

Even in ministry, we can get so involved in activities that we don't take time out to hear from the Lord. We need to ask ourselves if we, like Queen Vashti, are too busy celebrating what the King has given us to respond to His call? Or are we, like Queen Esther, approaching Him by faith, knowing that our life and the life of our people depend upon His favor? We will find that His scepter is always extended to us when we approach Him in humility and faith.

At the beginning of every year, our church sets aside a week for fasting and prayer, giving the year to the Lord and seeking His direction. In January 2000, I put all the programs in our church on hold so that we could bring them before the Lord for His fresh direction. This included the children's, adolescent, youth, ladies' and men's ministries; education, health, communications, intercession, prison and hospital ministries; RC (evangelistic dance troop), RC Jr., and more. We prayed over each one individually. Did the Lord lead us into this ministry, or were we just doing something that churches are expected to do? If He had lead us into this ministry, were we to continue? If so, were the people involved appointed by the Lord? Was the ministry going in the right direction?

This made some people a bit nervous. Perhaps their ministry would not continue! But I think it is wise to let go of our comfortable programs to hear what the Lord has to say about them. After all, it is not our church, but His.

This procedure is what led us some years earlier to start pastoral groups. Until then we had typical cell groups, but the Lord spoke to us. In obedience we raised up pastors who shepherded the groups at a deeper level than the original cell leaders. We had not seen this anywhere else. We simply followed the leading of the Holy Spirit. Structurally, it may not seem very different from the outside, but it was a wonderful turning point and strengthened our church.

Like David, we need to learn total dependence on the Lord so that His plans and purposes can be accomplished. We cannot compare one church or ministry to another. We need to know the Lord's will for us and walk in His will. Then unity can come as well, because we are doing what He has called us to do and allowing others to do the same. In the process, we will find we need one another.

To experience His glory and presence, we must hear from Him and follow His leading. We cannot do it our way. And how He chooses to work will be different in each city and church. We must all seek Him in humility, but the answers He gives us will be unique for our different needs. *God has the key to our cities. His plan is unique for each one. And He wants us to depend totally on Him, not on the plans or programs of men.* The Holy Spirit must tell us what to do, and we must remove the idols from the temple.

Being Accountable

Jesus was accountable to His Father. Before He died He gave a report to the Father saying, "I have brought You glory on earth by completing the work You gave Me to do" (John 17: 4). In the rest of this chapter Jesus relates all that He did in accord with the will of His Father. "I have revealed You…I gave them the words You gave me…I protected them and kept them safe…none has been lost except the one doomed to destruction…I have given them Your word…I have given them the glory that You gave Me…I have made You known to them and will continue to make You known" (verses 6, 8, 12, 14, 22, 26). Throughout these verses we can see that Jesus' measure of success was having done the will of His Father.

Jesus Himself explains, "Not everyone who says to Me, 'Lord, Lord,' will enter the kingdom of heaven, but only he *who does the will of My Father* who is in heaven" (Matthew 7:21). We may have a prophetic or deliverance ministry, or we may perform signs and wonders. But if our ministry was not authorized by the Lord and is not His will, we have nothing in the end. Anything less than His perfect will, even though it may have good results, will still fall short of what the Lord had in mind. We must remember that His ways and thoughts are higher than ours. We cannot allow ourselves to be satisfied with anything that does not satisfy Him.

He Hears the Cry of His People

Too often we forget just how close the Lord is to us, how quickly His heart is touched, and how much He longs to commune with us and move in our midst. When the children of Israel called out to the Lord in their anguish in Egypt, the Lord saw their misery, heard them crying out, and was concerned about their suffering, so He came down to bring them up (Exodus 3:7–9). How comforting to know that His heart responds to our circumstances and cries. At times, the circumstances of life become heavy, but prayer will reach His heart. "This is the one I esteem: he who is humble and contrite in spirit, and trembles at My word" (Isaiah 66:2).

In Luke 18 Jesus teaches us that persevering prayer will keep us from fainting in difficult times, for He will hear and answer.

Humility is the First Step to Bringing His Presence

Humility (dependence on the Lord) will result in obedience and holiness. This is what the Lord requires in His people. It is the first step to opening the gates of heaven for our lives, our cities, and our nations. In 2 Chronicles 16:9 we are told that the Lord searches for those whose hearts are fully committed to Him in order to show Himself strong on their behalf. He wants to show

Himself powerful so that those around us may be attracted to our Lord as well.

The Lord also promises that when we humble ourselves and bring ourselves under submission to Him, it will cause Him to move in our land. Scripture teaches us that the humility of His people is the first step towards city transformation (2 Chronicles 7:14). We need to humble ourselves, bringing ourselves down to subjection to Him and His will. Once we find humility, then we can effectively entreat the Lord and seek His face. Only then can we identify and turn from our wicked ways. And our ways are wicked, although they may be considered by society as good or religious ways.

Even successful programs can become wicked when they replace the Lord and His direction. We need to learn that a successful church or successful individual is one that is fulfilling the Lord's call. It may be a large church or a small one. It takes time to humble ourselves, to pray, and to seek His face in order to know His will. But we must partake of that manna.

There are many wicked ways from which we must turn. When we get into the heart of God for our churches and cities by humbly seeking Him and turning from our own ways, then the Lord will hear us and forgive us. And He will heal our land.

Enter His Rest

We must also learn to enter into His rest. The Lord lives in eternity, where there is no time. Everything He has in His heart for us and for our communities already exists in the heavenly realm. According to the book of Hebrews, there is a real tabernacle in the heavenlies where He dwells in majesty. That is why it was so important for Moses to construct the tabernacle exactly as the Lord instructed him. It was an earthly replica of what already existed in heaven. Moses was to bring this pattern down to earth.

Likewise, we are to bring God's will to earth. That's why Jesus taught His disciples to pray saying, "Your kingdom come, Your will be done on earth as it is in heaven" (Matthew 6:10). His will needs to be brought down to earth. We can say that Christian life is the means of plugging into the heavenly realm and bringing it down to earth. That is what the writer of Hebrews meant when he wrote about "entering his rest" (Hebrews 4:1–11). In a sense, it has already been done. God's rest consists of the good works that God "prepared in advance for us to do" (Ephesians 2:10).

We are no longer to strive to do something for the Lord. Unfortunately, many of us don't understand this. We're so busy working *for* God that we have no time to partner *with* God. We're so busy *working* for God that we have no time to *come into His presence*. As a result, we're not even doing the work of God.

The Sabbath rest was a sign, a weekly reminder, that Israel was dependent on God and not on human works. It was to be a constant reminder to them that their success was based on the favor of their God and obedience to Him. And today there is that same invitation to the church to enter into the Sabbath rest, desisting from our own works.

Humility, prayer, obedience, faith and holiness are all connected. Knowing that we are dependent on God will cause us to pray. As we do, the Lord speaks to us and gives us direction. As we obey, we put faith into action, infusing our lives with spiritual authority and power. Then, when hard times come, we have an endurance that can only come from on high, because He is the Lord of life. If we are submitted to Jesus Christ, dependent on Him and obedient, we will see the Lord do the impossible in our lives and communities. Daniel says, "...the people who know their God shall be strong, and carry out great exploits" (Daniel 11:32, NKJV).

Nothing brings down the glory of God's presence like humility—a total dependence on God alone. It means presenting ourselves as living sacrifices, leaving our own desires and plans to seek after God's. It means knowing that nothing else is worth living for.

We will never see the glory of God on earth unless we humble ourselves before the Lord, becoming totally dependent on Him, learning His ways, and doing His will.

Part III
The Goal of
UNITY

So that the World may Know

...that the world may know that You have sent Me... .
John 17:23, NKJV

If we make unity the goal for the churches of our community, we have missed the purpose of the Lord. Unity is not an end in itself but a means to an end. Genesis 11 clearly shows that unity has a purpose. As we noted earlier, the LORD Himself comments about this in verse 6: "...then nothing they plan to do will be impossible for them." The purpose of unity is to accomplish a plan. In this particular case, people who had rejected God designed a building project to exalt man and make a name for themselves.

The source of all plans will either be man or God. It is up to us to choose the source. Jesus, through His sacrifice on the cross, worked in perfect unity with the Father and the Holy Spirit to provide a way for us to have restored fellowship with the Godhead. He made the way for us to enter the kingdom of God. But this salvation is not simply for us as individuals; it is for our communities as well. When we understand this, we can seek God's will for reaching our particular communities or cities with the gospel.

The Scriptures teach two avenues for spreading the gospel: extension and attraction. The first requires the church to go out to the nations. The second requires the nations to come into the church.

Evangelism by Extension

We are more familiar with extension, which is the church reaching out to others. We think of mission work as evangelistic outreach. From the days of the early church, there have been outreach ministries. Over 300 years ago William Carey, the "Father of Modern Day Missions," started missionary work in India. And today we have evangelistic outreaches ranging from casual witness (to a relative, friend or neighbor), to coordinated door-to-door campaigns, to large crusades in football stadiums, to the use of mass media. In each case the church is reaching out, or extending itself, to present the gospel. We base this ministry on Matthew 28:18: "Go ye therefore...."

Even though extension can be effective apart from the city-church, a united effort wonderfully facilitates the reaching of a community. As a united church in Cali, we have learned that service to the community is an effective means of evangelism, but we have also seen thousands respond to the gospel through the preaching of the Word in large crusades. The city-church can reach the community in ways that a single ministry or church cannot.

After we started praying as a united church, the gospel began to penetrate all stratas of society. As professionals began coming to the Lord, they wanted to serve Him with their knowledge and abilities. Those who worked in the health field formed a medical foundation designed to serve the Christian community with affordable medical services. They established a health insurance plan that offers good care at reasonable prices. But they needed a place for their medical offices and services.

The Lord was at work preparing that place. A man in prison was wonderfully saved and wanted to serve the Lord. He had already built a large hospital in the southern part of the city, and after being released from prison he offered the eighth floor of his clinic for the Christian medical foundation! This served them for the first couple of years of their ministry.

But serving the people of God was not enough for the medical foundation. These men and women wanted to serve their city as well. They began by forming mobile medical teams to go into the poorer sections of town, offering their services free of charge. They asked *"Jesus en las Calles,"* our city-church evangelistic team, to join them. Today, as the medical team offers its professional services, the evangelistic team shares the gospel! Many people have come to the Lord through this ministry.

At the end of the year 2000, the medical foundation sent its statistics to the city's Department of Health showing how many children had been vaccinated and how many people had been treated for parasites. The Department responded with a request that they check their data; there seemed to be some mistake. But there was no mistake. To everyone's surprise, the Christian medical team had vaccinated more children and treated more people for parasites than the city's Department of Health!

Together, we are able to reach into our communities in effective ways.

I have already shared how the Lord has given us *TeleUnidad*, the first Christian television station in Colombia. That station was one of the fruits of unity among believers in our city. But like the medical mission, we also needed space, a large area for producing programs and setting up offices. However, our budget was far below what we needed to acquire adequate space.

But the Lord performed a miracle! The same man who had rented the eighth floor to the medical foundation offered us the eleventh floor of the hospital—at an incredibly reduced price! Because it is the top floor, it gave us access to the terraced roof, giving us a 360-degree view of Cali—the perfect backdrop for productions!

The biggest surprise came when we saw the eleventh floor. It had copper pipes, marble floors, beautiful wooden closets, an enormous bar, a spa, a beauty parlor, and much more. This floor of the building had been designed as a refuge for people escaping the authorities; it allowed them to posture as patients in a "hospital" while enjoying all the luxuries they could possibly want! But the Lord never permitted the eleventh floor be used for anything other than the Christian television station. The bar now serves as a beautiful reception desk. Each room is wonderfully designed for our needs. Only the Lord could have provided for us in such a wonderful way!

TeleUnidad's purpose is to offer programs that uphold and encourage values and principles in a city more accustomed to being targeted with sexual promiscuity, nudity and violence in its TV programs. The Christian programming is directed towards the needs of our society. We are not advertising churches but offering people wholesome television—showing a better way for themselves and their children.

As we work together in unity, we can accomplish things that would not be possible alone. But we must remember that unity is fragile. It demands humility, our complete dependence on the Lord, obedience to His Word, prayer, a search for His purposes, a godly perspective, and perseverance. We cannot become satisfied and fall into complacency. We must learn to press into Him and we will find that the Lord will always do more as we seek Him.

Extension Through Continental Unity

Unity reaches beyond city and national borders. We are now beginning to experience unity in His international body. We see this, for example, in the Iberoamerican Confederation of Christian Communicators and Mass Media (COICOM, or simply "the Confederation" for present purposes). This organization has brought together communicators from broad and diverse denominational backgrounds throughout the Spanish-speaking world. The Confederation's mission is to help Christian communicators achieve excellence, efficiency, integrity, and unity.

It encourages them to find more effective and creative ways to communicate the gospel to produce societal change, and fulfillment of the Great Commission is accelerated.

The Confederation's president, Raul Justiniano, is a well-known communicator and international speaker who teaches on leadership, excellence, and efficiency. It is all too rare in my experience to find businessmen who are given to prayer, fasting and seeking the Lord. Raul is one of these men.

With a burden for reaching our nations with the gospel, the Confederation started its *Plan 1,000 Dias* ("Plan of 1,000 Days") in April of 1998. The goal is to reach 600 million Spanish-speaking inhabitants in 26 countries and 300 cities with the gospel of Jesus Christ. This will be accomplished by mobilizing the church and the mass media, Christian and secular, to work together to saturate the region with the gospel in a span of 1,000 days.

The 1,000-Day Plan is flexible and open and each city is encouraged to follow the direction of the Lord for itself. In fact, the Plan starts with months of prayer and fasting and goes on to include evangelism, discipleship, church planting, and missions. The three pillars of the Plan are (1) prayer and fasting, as we humble ourselves before the Lord, (2) a great sowing, involving the mass media, and (3) the great harvest. During the first year Raul traveled extensively, teaching on humility and prayer and promoting coordinated, continental fasts of 10, 21, and 40 days.

At one point, several nations met at the same time for united prayer throughout Central and South America. Some gathered in churches, others in fields, coliseums or stadiums. From Cali's stadium we called Quito, Ecuador, for radio coverage and San Jose, Costa Rica, for television coverage. Others called in from their cities as well with reports like these: "There are so many (whatever the number was) here in Lima, Peru, praying this night." "There are so many here in Cali...Buenos Aires...." What an inspiration it was to know that believers from different countries were seeking the Lord in a special way at the same time throughout the continent!

The *vigilias* in Cali have served as an example and encouragement for others in united prayer. Materials and projects from other countries have served as a stimulus elsewhere. Guatemala, for example, made excellent one-minute television and radio spots promoting Judeo-Christian standards; these have now been used in other countries. Together we have produced videos, manuals, and a national and international "Winners of Cities" seminar for pastors and leaders.

Many Christian ministries participate in these massive outreaches—Campus Crusade, the *Jesus* film, the Bible Society, Latin America via Satellite, HCJB, Christian Broadcasting Network, and Semilla (Seed). Prominent Christian leaders have also participated, including: Alberto Motessi, Hermano Pablo, Marco Barrientos, Claudio Freidson, Marco Witt, Danilo Montero, and many others.

As we pray and work together we have seen the Lord do incredible things. In Potosi, Bolivia, during the summer of 2001, 80 percent of the population was reached with the gospel. There were 35,000 decisions for Christ—20 percent of the population! In Peru, several cities will have been reached with the gospel by the end of 2001. And in November of 2002, Christians are planning a simultaneous outreach to Lima and other Peruvian cities. Babahoyo and four other cities in Ecuador were reached this year. In July of 2002, the 3.5 million inhabitants of Guayaquil will be reached with the gospel.

In 2001, at the Confederation's annual conference held in Santa Cruz, Bolivia, an average of 20,000 people attended evening meetings in the stadium as millions watched on national and international television or listened on the radio. The Confederation has proven to be a great motivator for unity and vision among pastors and religious leaders.

The united church is able to take the gospel to whole communities in large regions. Unity now reaches beyond the borders of our city or our country; it embraces the body of Christ throughout the world. There is an inherent strength when we work in unity with many ministries from different countries and denominations. And we must work while it is yet day, for the night will come when no man can work (John 9:4).

Evangelism by Attraction

The second avenue for spreading the gospel is by attracting the nations to the church by her unique lifestyle. Although this was well understood by Israel, it calls for a paradigm shift for most of us. *"The nations shall know that I am the LORD," declares the Sovereign LORD, "when I show myself holy through you before their eyes"* (Ezekiel 36:23b). This demands much more commitment than extension—taking the message to others—and requires a united church. It is the kingdom of God made visible, and we are still learning just what that means.

Kingdom life is what will attract the nations to our Lord. Bringing the salvation message, that is, seeing people saved and grounding them in the Word, is only part of what the Lord has in His heart. We need to understand and live the kingdom of God.

The kingdom of God is emphasized throughout the New Testament. In fact, the kingdom is mentioned more than 100 times in the Gospels alone. It was John the Baptist's message to prepare the way of the Lord. Later Jesus taught many lessons about the kingdom, and the same message continued throughout the early church. Jesus' message during the 40 days after His resurrection was about the kingdom of God (Acts 1:2–4). The apostles preached the same message: Philip in Samaria, Paul and Barnabas on their missionary journey, Paul in Ephesus and Rome (Acts 8:12; 14:22–24; 19:8; 28:23–31). Paul also writes about the kingdom of God in Romans, 1 Corinthians, Galatians, Ephesians, Colossians, 1 and 2 Thessalonians, and 2 Timothy. The kingdom of God is also presented by James, Peter and the writer to the Hebrews. Finally, John in the book of Revelation speaks of the day when the kingdom of this world will become the kingdom of our Lord and of his Christ (Revelation 11:15).

The kingdom of God is not the church, although the church is part of the kingdom. In the kingdom, God reigns. The kingdom of God reflects the character of our Lord to the nations around us.

The Nations, Jesus' Inheritance

The nations are Jesus' inheritance (Psalm 2:8). Before Jesus ascended, He commanded us to "disciple the nations" (Matthew 28:18). Although "nations" can be used as a more generic term, meaning the heathen, I believe the word used here refers to people groups. It is the same Greek word used by the Jews who told Jesus that the centurion loved their "nation." Throughout the Old and New Testaments we see the prophetic word of judgment on cities and nations—and blessing on those who accept the word.

The first mention of nations in the Bible is found in Genesis 10:5, where the term is also defined. A nation is a group of people who are from the same bloodline, or who speak the same language, or are from the same land or territory. Using the same Hebrew word, Isaiah and other prophets speak of the nations coming to the church:

> Arise, shine, for your light has come, and the glory of the Lord
> rises upon you. See, darkness covers the earth and thick
> darkness is over the peoples, but the LORD rises upon you and
> His glory appears over you. Nations will come to your light,
> and kings to the brightness of your dawn.
> Isaiah 60:1–3

God established the nations and set times for them so that they would seek His face. In Acts 17:26–27 Paul says:

> From one man He made every nation of men, that they should
> inhabit the whole earth; and He determined the times set for
> them and the exact places where they should live. God did this
> so that men would seek Him and perhaps reach out for Him and
> find Him…

No matter what political arrangements have been made or what wars have been waged in forming the nations, it is God who has purposefully set the boundaries of the nations and has determined set times for them. During the last several decades many new nations have been established. God's reason for this is so that men will seek Him. He wants the nations to seek His face! We can easily see that if the nations are going to be attracted to the church, as it says in Isaiah 60, we must be a people united in the Lord and living in the power of His kingdom. No individual church, ministry or denomination can fully reflect our Lord and teach the nations His ways. Together we are to have the answer for the nations of the world, to be light for those who are living in great darkness. There are several examples of this in the Old Testament.

Solomon is a type of the church. 1 Kings 10:1 refers to the Queen of Sheba's visit. She came not only because of Solomon's wisdom but "because she heard about Solomon's wisdom *in relation to his Lord.*" The nations around him saw, through Solomon, the God who gave him wisdom. The Queen of Sheba went to ask him hard questions, to which she received good answers.

When the heathen Babylonians heard how the Lord had healed Hezekiah, and of the miraculous sign of the sun returning ten degrees, they went to see for themselves. Unfortunately, instead of leading them to the One responsible for these miracles, Hezekiah showed off all his earthly possessions. As a result, he not only lost a wonderful opportunity to lift up the name of the Lord but, in the end, lost his possessions as well.

When the fingers appeared and wrote a message on the palace wall, Belshazzar was so affected that his countenance changed, his thoughts were troubled, and his knees knocked so hard that he couldn't stand. But the queen mother remembered Daniel as a man in the kingdom with the "spirit of the holy gods in him." She knew that he would have an answer when no one else did. That is the way the church should be seen by society—the one with an answer because the Spirit of God dwells within her.

The nations are looking for answers. The church of Jesus Christ needs to have answers for society's hard questions. While the earth is in deep darkness, the church is to show forth light so that the nations will be attracted to our Lord (Isaiah 60:1–3). Could the darkness to which Isaiah refers be the same as the night that Jesus speaks about in John 9:4, the night in which no one can work?

How Do We Disciple Nations?

We need to remember that the Lord's intention was that Adam would live in a beautiful garden. He had a "garden culture" in mind, a lifestyle that would produce health and strength, and most of all, assure close communion between God and man.

With the fall, the Lord's purposes were not thwarted. God chose Abraham and, from his seed, made a nation called Israel. Israel would be His people and He would be their God. God would walk among His people and dwell with them. No other nation has experienced the miraculous deliverance, protection, and provision as this nation whose God was the Lord. The lifestyle of its people was to reflect the God they loved and served, thus becoming a light to the Gentiles (Isaiah 49:6).

Sadly, Israel was enamored with the heathen nations and took on their way of life. Over and again, the Lord sent prophets to call Israel back to Himself. At times, they repented and had a revival, but Israel as a nation kept compromising her calling.

Even though Israel failed, the Lord made a way for her to come back to Himself and, at the same time, opened the doors for the Gentiles to find salvation. Through the death, resurrection and ascension of Jesus, the Father provided that way. The Lord revealed to Paul that believing Gentiles are heirs together with believing Israelites and are members of one body. Those who believe have become a "chosen people, a royal priesthood, a holy nation, a people belonging to God" (1 Peter 2:9–10). The church of Jesus Christ, the body of Christ, the bride of Christ, is intended to reflect the person of God.

The church is God's instrument to bring change to earth. We

are the salt of the earth, the light of the world. In 2 Kings 2:19–22 we read that Jericho was located in a beautiful place. However, the water was bad, affecting the ground and apparently causing miscarriages. When the men of the city told Elisha about the problem, he threw salt into the source of the water and the waters were healed. Today, the church is to be that salt, preserving and healing our communities. However, if we lose our saltiness, we lose our influence in the world and are to be thrown out and trampled upon (Matthew 5:13).

We must have an answer for society, but unfortunately most of us were raised in the philosophies of "Egypt" and have much more of the world's way of thinking in our lives than we realize. When we come to the Lord for salvation, we usually deal with sin and sometimes with healing and deliverance. But we don't usually talk about being saved from "this perverse generation." We live with the same worldly philosophy that most of us learned from our parents and our "Egyptian" school system.

As a result, there is often too little difference between the world and the church. Compounding the problem, many Christians don't even realize that there should be a difference, a difference that will change our communities, not just our individual lives. Too often we have said, like Israel, "We want to be like the nations, like the peoples of the world who serve wood and stone"—or in our case, money and pleasure (Ezekiel 20:32). "Foreigners have entered the holy places of the Lord's house" (Jeremiah 51:51). At times the visions of the prophets are "worthless" because they do not expose sin. Or the priests do not distinguish between the holy and common (Lamentations 2:14).

The Lord is in the process of cleansing His church from the "Egyptian" ways, just as He cleansed Israel in the desert. Peter tells us that we were redeemed from the empty way of life handed down to us from our fathers (1 Peter 1:18). Paul says that we have died with Christ to the basic principles of this world (Colossians 2:20). As we begin to understand the ways of God, our minds are renewed and we become transformed.

We are hindered in our understanding of God's ways and

purposes by preconceived ideas, mindsets, and paradigms that do not have their roots in the Lord, but rather in the world. We must examine these to determine if they are among the "strongholds"— arguments and pretensions that set themselves up against the knowledge of God—that the Apostle Paul tells us we must demolish. Every thought must be brought into submission and obedience to Christ (2 Corinthians 10:4, 5).

Life is not separated into the secular and religious. Life is one. Jesus is the way, the truth, and the life. By Him and for Him all things were created. In Him all things are held together (Colossians 1:15–20). These are not just nice Scripture verses. They are truths that, once grasped, will change the very way we think and live. They are the basis for a biblical worldview. They affect how we see our cities, nations, and world.

The church has the message of salvation through the blood of Jesus and repentance of sins. But we need a message that covers more than just our spiritual needs. Certainly we can see that God is interested in our whole lives as individuals and communities. But we haven't been taught about life the way God intended it to be. What did God originally have in mind for us? How should life be lived, as far as He is concerned?

Jesus teaches us in the Gospels about issues of the heart and soul. Because He has made a way, our calling is yet higher than that of the Old Testament. In Matthew 5, Jesus gives us standards that go beyond the law. Our righteousness must exceed the righteousness of the Pharisees. He tells us that it is not only sin to commit adultery but even sin to look at a woman with lust. The Christian life demands a higher standard than does the Law because it deals with the heart, not only actions. And God has given us His indwelling Holy Spirit to make it possible to live a holy life, pleasing in His sight (Philippians 2:13).

The Lord is interested in every area of our lives. We can see this in the teachings of Jesus as well as in the Law of Moses. Let's consider the latter. This is not a suggestion that we return to the Law, for we are no longer under it, but we can see how Israel was to live in order to reflect Jehovah God to the nations around them.

The Law required the Israelites to live according to standards set by the Lord. These standards apply to their conquests, feasts, sacrifices, thank offerings, marriages, government, kings and judicial system, inheritances, treatment of pagans, and more. The Law dealt with personal rights, remedies, health and dietary laws, social welfare, and other areas of life. God is interested in the family, politics, education, agriculture, communications, and more. In other words, He is to reign in every area.

As a church we need to discover God's thoughts and ways. This calls for study and openness on our part, and demands major paradigm shifts. When Jesus taught that the Sabbath was made for man and not vice versa, this was an enormous paradigm shift for the Jews. Only those who are born-again can see the things of the kingdom of God.

We need to learn the philosophy of the kingdom of God in all areas of life. Christians are actively working together today to develop a Christian philosophy of government, politics, economic development, business management, social welfare, and so forth. For example, in our approach to helping the poor, we tend to make them dependent on us or on the government, but that is not God's intention. He is interested in maturing the individual, developing his character, and giving him dignity. The Old Testament Law called for actions that helped the poor to become financially independent.

Kingdom life does not depend on academic achievements, but on obedience to the ways of God. As a modern example, consider Almolonga, Guatemala. God has given this community a piece of the "garden culture." The people lack the academic knowledge that we would ordinarily think necessary to produce an increase in harvests of 1,000 percent in a short period of time. Yet they attracted the attention of the United States Department of Agriculture, which investigated this phenomenon. We have seen similar increases in harvests in Peru and other areas of Guatemala where entire communities have embraced the gospel.

When we study the area of health, we soon discover that we have deviated greatly from the principles for maintaining health.

With the germ theory, the Western world began turning its back on understanding the factors that affect the susceptibility of the host and, instead, developed a whole medical system based on a pharmacological approach. This has resulted in a false freedom to indulge in a lifestyle of doing what "feels good" or eating whatever our appetite demands, without self-control or proper exercise, rest, and nutrition. But this "freedom" has made us a drug dependent society. We take over-the-counter and prescribed drugs to relieve the symptoms and diseases that we have brought upon ourselves. We ignore the fact that the Lord created man so that he could maintain health and fight disease by living in accordance with natural laws. In ignorance, we break these laws and suffer the consequences. This does not mean that medicines do not have their place, but that we have become all too drug-oriented in search of quick remedies.

Those of us in developing countries can appreciate these matters in a special way. Many in these counties can't afford medical attention, nor do they have health insurance. Some will save money for months to have the funds to consult a medical doctor. If he gives them a prescription, their visit has been in vain because they can't afford the prescribed drug. However, God's natural laws are available to all.

This does not mean that medical doctors are not important and necessary, but simply that we need a change of thinking in this area. We over-emphasize drugs, severing the connection between the spiritual and the physical. I believe there are many false assumptions in this area, but God has raised up professionals that have answers that glorify God and bring the whole area of health into a biblical perspective.

In the last 30 years or so, Christian education has come into the foreground. Initially, many considered it a way to protect their children from the world. Today, Christians are realizing that true education must be centered on the One in whom all things consist. True education gives us an understanding of God's character and ways. Science permits us to discover more of the greatness of our infinite God. History is no longer the story of man, but "His story"—God's dealings with man. We learn how He prepared the world for the coming Messiah, how He has dealt with the nations, how He has given them opportunities to receive Him, and how He judges them on the basis of their response. We also see how their response affected art and literature.

During these last decades the Lord has raised up people to work in this area, as seen in A Beka, Rod and Staff, Accelerated Christian Education, Bill Gothard's curriculum, and others. Not every church or ministry needs to write curriculum. God has already raised up these ministries to bless the body of Christ. But we do need to understand the Christian philosophy of education that they have learned from the Lord.

Man has invented many wonderful instruments and tools that serve mankind. All of these things are meant to expand His kingdom and glorify God, yet men have corrupted them. Mass media is to be a means of communicating God's majesty and works throughout the earth. Yet it is one of the most powerful tools used by the enemy to promulgate sin. Again we find that the Lord has raised up men of God with a biblical perspective in this area. Rigoberto Manuel Galvez has written a book about the theology of communications that brings this area into a balanced, godly perspective.

God is raising people in areas of education, government, social welfare, communications, etc., and when we work together, all that knowledge and experience is brought together to benefit the kingdom of God and society. We will find that He gives us answers for the hard questions. The nations will be attracted to a church whose lifestyle and culture reflects and glorifies their God.

This is true within cities and countries and even globally. It is time to work together to see His kingdom come, and for His will to be done on earth as it is in heaven. For too long we have been busy building our own houses (churches and denominations).

How much will be accomplished before the return of the Lord Jesus? We really don't know. But we do know that we are to "occupy till He comes." As a united church we have a huge task set before us to define what life in the kingdom is—and to live it.

Just as the Israelites needed to spend more than a year in the desert learning the ways of the Lord, which were contrary to the ways of Egypt, so too, we must learn how to live in all areas of life. No one church or group is going to have all the answers. As we come together in unity, we will find that the Lord has given understanding to each of us in different areas. Together we will find the answers that we need to live according to His ways.

In Ephesians 1:17, 18, Paul says, "I keep asking that the God of our Lord Jesus Christ, the glorious Father may give you a spirit of wisdom and revelation so that you may know Him better. I pray also, that the eyes of your heart may be enlightened in order that you may know the hope to which He has called you, *the riches of His glorious inheritance in the saints*, and His incomparable great power to us who believe."

We need revelation to understand the glorious inheritance that Jesus has in His saints. Until He gives us revelation of the manifold diversity of His body, we won't have unity as we should. And as we unite, we will receive the mind of Christ. He is our wisdom. When we are united, we will have the glory of the Lord. And the nations will be attracted to our Lord.

"The nations shall know that I am the Lord, when I show Myself holy through you before their eyes" (Ezekiel 36:23).

Our prayer must be His own: "Thy kingdom come, Thy will be done on earth as it is in heaven."

All the ends of the earth will remember and turn to the LORD,
and all the families of the nations will bow down before Him, for
dominion belongs to the LORD and He rules over the nations.
Psalm 22:27–28

✒ Lord, make us one so that the world will know You.

Julio C. Ruibal Foundation

For more information on Ruth Ruibal and the work in Cali, Colombia, or additional resources, you may contact her at:

The Julio C. Ruibal Foundation
P.O. Box 1830
Pinellas Park, FL 33780-1830
USA

www.ruibal.org

The Julio C. Ruibal Foundation invites you to become part of their ministry which is so effectively impacting and strengthening the church at large and reaching out to the lost. First, we ask you to pray for the Ruibal family. But we also ask you to become involved in what the Lord is doing by standing with them financially. You can be part of this dynamic ministry as you pray and give.

The Julio C. Ruibal Foundation is a nonprofit religious corporation founded by Julio and Ruth Ruibal in 1985. All donations are tax deductible.

For more information on The Sentinel Group or additional available resources, you may contact us at:

The Sentinel Group
P.O. Box 6334
Lynnwood, WA 98036
USA

1-800-668-5657
www.TransformNations.com